ENDLESS QUEST

Where Is My Dad At?

VIVIENNE D'AMOUR

Copyright © 2024 Vivienne D'amour
All Rights Reserved

No part of this publication may be reproduced or distributed in any form or by any means without the prior permission of the author and/or publisher.

Kemp House
152 -160 City Road
London, EC1V 2NX
United Kingdom

ISBN: 978-1-917451-18-5

Published by Vivienne D'amour and Action Wealth Publishing

Printed and bound in the United Kingdom

Scripture quotations taken from The Holy Bible, New International Version® NIV® Copyright © 1973, 1978, 1984, 2011 by Biblica, Inc. Used with permission. All rights reserved worldwide.

Scripture quotations marked (KJV) are taken from the KING JAMES VERSION, public domain.
Scripture quotations are taken from the Holy Bible, New Living Translation, copyright ©1996, 2004, 2015 by Tyndale House Foundation. Used by permission of Tyndale House Publishers, Carol Stream, Illinois 60188. All rights reserved.

Although the author and publisher have made every effort to ensure the accuracy and completeness of information contained in this book, we assume no responsibility for errors, inaccuracies, omissions, or any inconsistency herein. Any slights on people, places, or organizations are unintentional.

The material in this book is provided for educational purposes only. No responsibility for loss occasioned to any person or corporate body acting or refraining to act as a result of reading material in this book can be accepted by the author or publisher.

In today's fast-paced world, we often forget to pause and reflect on how our actions or words affect others. Life becomes a race to complete tasks and tick off to-do lists, leaving little room for genuine connection. But life is not just about accomplishments; it is about the moments we share, the experiences that shape us, and the impact we leave behind.

This book invites you to slow down and consider the untold stories of those around you, the child whose struggles you may not see, the person you've loved, helped, or perhaps judged. Every child is unique, and while my story is personal, it offers a glimpse into what children, particularly those from single-parent households or who have experienced loss, might be thinking and feeling as they navigate life's challenges. I have been deeply hurt watching some mothers deny fathers access to their children. It is equally shocking to see some fathers go weeks, even months, living their lives breathing, eating, and carrying on without knowing anything about their children's lives.

Through my journey, I reflect on the lingering questions about my father's absence, the blend of hope and heartbreak in my encounters with him, and the lessons from my relationships with other men. I share my path of reconciliation, the gift of receiving my father's final blessing, and the healing that followed. It took immense courage to write this, and I hope these reflections will resonate with you, offering understanding and perhaps even helping to save or guide someone along the way.

ENDLESS QUEST

CONTENTS

NOTE TO THE AUTHOR 13
PREFACE 14
FOREWORD 18
ACKNOWLEDGMENTS 20
INTRODUCTION 23
CHAPTER ONE 25
THE UNSEEN DAD 25
    Growing Up Without a Dad 25
    Life in Kyabazaala Village 27
    Fear and Absence of a Father Figure 29
CHAPTER TWO 31
TRACING SHADOWS 31
    Learning About a Father for the First Time 31
    Meeting my Dad for the First Time 32
    Unmet Expectations and Growing
        Disappointment 33
    Lessons from a Complicated Father-Daughter
        Relationship 34
CHAPTER THREE 40
BROKEN EARLY 40

    The Pain of Rejection 40
    Searching for Fulfillment 41
    Carving My Horn Through Friendships:
        Friendships That Shaped Me 42
    Fighting My Way Through 43

CHAPTER FOUR 46

THROUGH SPIRITUAL FATHERS 46

    Struggling to Relate to God as a Father 46
    Finding, Comfort, and Inspiration in Church 47
    Choosing Reconciliation over Resentment 49
    The Missing Blueprint of Love 50
    Relationships 51
    Unhealthy Love and Misplaced Expectations 52

CHAPTER FIVE 56

BACK TO REALITY 56

    Endless Quest for Fathers 56
    Placement 57
    Loss and the Final Blessing 58
    It Is Not a Want – The Irreplaceable Role of a
        Father 59
    Emotional Scars and Their Long-Term Impact . 60
    Relationship Challenges 61
    Identity Formation 62
    Educational and Career Challenges 62
    Behavioral Issues 63

- Negative Coping Mechanisms That Shape Our Lives 63
- Breaking the Cycle Through Awareness and Support 66

CHAPTER SIX 71
GOD'S IDEA 71

- Marriage 72
- You're His Own 74
- Children Are A Blessing 75
- My Reflections Concerning Children 77
- God Is a God of Order 77
- Work It Out 80
- In the Way They Should Go 82
- New/ Blended Families 84
- Just Be a Parent: Stop Trying to Be a Super-mom or Super-dad 86

CHAPTER SEVEN 90
FATHERHOOD 90

- Absent Dads 90
- The Emotionally Absent Father: A Silent Wound 91
- Moving Forward: Bridging the Emotional Gap 92
- The Abusive Father: A Source of Harm 92
- Father Figures 94
- Importance of a Father Figure for Daughters 95
- I am an Adopted Grandchild 97

Three Lessons I Treasure 100
Fatherlessness in Uganda and the USA: Facts,
    Causes, and Impacts 101
Fatherlessness in the United States 104

CHAPTER EIGHT 107

THE FATHER WOUND 107

Understanding Father Wounds in Men 107
Characteristics of Men with Father Wounds 108
Healing Father Wounds: Steps Toward
    Restoration 109
The Father Wound in Women 111
How Father Wounds Manifest in Women 112
Healing From Father Wounds 114
Conclusion: Stepping Into Wholeness 116

CHAPTER NINE 118

MY FATHERHOOD MODELS 118

CHAPTER TEN 128

CHILDHOOD TRAUMA 128

Recognizing the Ripple Effect of Unhealed
    Trauma 128
Taking Responsibility 129
What Is Childhood Trauma? 129
Personal Encounters with Trauma 130
The Long-Term Impact of Childhood Trauma . 131
Recovering from Childhood Trauma 132
Parents, Do Not Provoke Your Children 136

Struggles after School 138
The Role of Parents in Shaping Children's Futures 139
The Consequences of Neglect 140
Breaking the Cycle 140
Conclusion: Trusting in God's Process 141

CHAPTER ELEVEN 143

MOTHERS/LADIES 143

Navigating Emotions and Their Impact 143
Understanding Emotions 144
Breaking the Cycle 150
Breaking the Rules and Finding Freedom 153
Authority and Respect 154
The Need for Balanced Parenting 154
The Role of Parents in a Babysitter-Dependent World 157
The Value of Appreciation 157

CHAPTER TWELVE 160

BE DELIBERATE—MAKE TIME 160

Parenting through Changing Lenses 161

CHAPTER THIRTEEN 164

FAMILY AND RELATIONSHIPS 164

The Day I Cried Out to My Mum 164
Friendships over Family 165
A Wake-Up Call 165

The Importance of Investing in Family 166
Friendships and Relationships as Young Adult
.... 166
Breaking Cycles and Moving Forward 167
Reflections from My Dysfunctional Romantic
  Relationships 169
Toxicity Rooted in Our Past 172
Recognizing Emotional Abuse and Narcissism 173
Narcissism in Relationships 173
Celebrating Love and Acknowledging Pain 175
The Decision to Break Away 175
Hard Lessons about Love and Relationships ... 176
Healing and Growth 177
The Power of Sisterhood 179
Taking Breaks and Seeking God 179
Rediscovering Self-Worth 179
Embracing Self-Acceptance Amidst Change 184
Transitions in Relationships 185
Lessons on Change 186
Boundaries 187
Understanding Boundaries in Relationships ... 189
Conclusion: Navigating Life's Changes with Faith
.... 191

CHAPTER FOURTEEN 192
FORGIVENESS 192
The Meaning of Forgiveness 193

Forgiveness as Dying to Self 193
The Role of God's Servants in My Healing 194
Forgiveness Comes with Wisdom 195
The Power of Letting Go 196
I Took Back My Power 196
The Cost of Suppressed Pain 198
Confronting Anger and Finding Freedom 199
Reclaiming My Power 199
Taking Back Your Power 200

CHAPTER FIFTEEN 201

LETTERS OF THE HEART TO AND FROM THE CONCERNED 201

Living a Life That Writes Its Own Story 211

EPILOGUE 1 213

IMPACT OF DADS THROUGH MY FRIENDS' EYES .. 213

Conclusion 242
God, Our Perfect Father 244

EPILOGUE 2 247

INSPIRATION FOR FATHERS 247

Quotes That Define Fathers and Their Influence
.... 249

EPILOGUE 3 251

LET US PRAY FOR FATHERHOOD AND THE FATHERLESS 251

CONCLUSION 252

CALL TO ACTION 252
ABOUT THE AUTHOR 253

NOTE TO THE AUTHOR

Dear Vivienne,

I am beyond excited and honored to be part of your journey as you write this book. It's amazing to witness your passion for spreading the love of Christ and how your life radiates His love in everything you do. Your heart for the community, your love for people, and your commitment to sharing the gospel inspire many, me included. You've always been a shining example of selflessness, generosity, and kindness.

You touch hearts meaningfully through your beautiful voice, words, and deep, edifying conversations. I do not doubt that this book will reflect your incredible light and wisdom. Keep shining, keep sharing, and keep being the amazing disciple of Christ that you are. May this book bless all who read it, just as you are to us who know you.

With love, gratitude, and prayers for your continued success,

Chorm Cathy

PREFACE

I believe God allows certain experiences in our lives to foster personal growth and to reveal His greater purpose through us.
As He teaches and molds us, we are called to reflect His love and work to the world as He permits and leads us.

You learn so much after years of closely relating with any community, their way of life, beliefs, struggles, and strengths. I have had enough time to learn a lot in the past seven years as I closely interacted with my Ugandan community in Boston. One of the greatest issues I found we suffer that continually breaks my heart is the strife between men and women, particularly regarding their children. The reality of "baby daddy" and "baby mama" drama is all too real, and I have seen its impact firsthand.

It is heartbreaking to see some mothers deny fathers access to their children and equally shocking to witness fathers go weeks or even months without engaging in their children's lives. Do we realize the deeper impact of these actions? When a father refuses to take a call from his child's mother, it is not just her he's hurting. It is the child, too. A child's well-being is deeply tied to her mother's well-being. Likewise, when a mother denies a father the chance to see his child or lets bitterness consume her, it damages the child's relationship with their father. Allowing a father to be present isn't about him but about giving the child the connection they need.

Coming from a broken family, this issue weighs heavily on my heart. I have spoken to others about the effects of growing up without a father's presence. Some have listened, but others have dismissed me, accusing me of meddling. Despite this, I cannot turn a blind eye. I'm here for the future generations of children caught in the middle of their parents' unresolved differences.

Finding my voice on this issue has taken me years, but I now see how God has been at work. I do not have all the answers; I only have my story and lessons to share. Yet, my story can resonate with others and offer hope. From Boston to the world, God is working to restore families, starting with you and me. He desires to build stronger families today more than ever before.

As the Bible says, *"There is nothing new under the sun."* No experience is unique, but that does not mean we truly understand it. I share my life experiences so that fathers may see how deeply their children need them beyond financial support and drama. Children long for emotional connection with their fathers. Your presence isn't a luxury; it is a necessity.

The rejection of a father leaves lasting emotional scars, affecting a child's self-worth and identity well into adulthood. Studies consistently show the devastating impact of fatherlessness: lower educational attainment, higher unemployment, increased poverty, and emotional struggles that persist for years. For example, 85% of incarcerated youth and 70% of adolescent substance abusers come from fatherless homes. This absence also leads to challenges in forming healthy relationships, trust issues, and higher rates of depression and anxiety. These statistics underscore fathers' irreplaceable role in shaping their children's lives and futures.

The absence of a father's love creates a void children often spend a lifetime trying to fill. This quest for validation can lead to destructive behaviors, perpetuating cycles of pain across generations.

This book is my effort to speak to those grappling with broken relationships with their parents. I know the pain personally, but I also know the healing power of God. It is not His will that you grew up broken or remain broken. God wants to give you a fresh start and heal your trauma. Hebrews 12:14 urges: *"Make every effort to live in peace with everyone and to be holy; without holiness, no one will see the Lord."* Peace, forgiveness, and love are at the heart of God's plan for our lives. Forgiveness is not about excusing past hurt but setting ourselves free from bitterness.

One of our generation's greatest challenges is fatherlessness; it is heartbreaking to see this cycle continue. But it does not have to. It is time to stop, reflect on the patterns in our families, and invite God to bring the change we need. By putting aside egos, bitterness, and selfishness, we can create a foundation for future generations to thrive. It begins with you and me.

This book isn't about placing blame or expressing ingratitude. My family knows how much I appreciate them and all they've done for me. My mother, especially, protected and provided for us in ways that were never done for her. Through her sacrifices, I have learned the importance of doing better for my children and future generations. Advocacy for children is not limited to my family; it is a calling to fight for all children, which I hope and pray we all can embrace.

I hope my story inspires you to reflect on how you can connect with your children. While babysitters and caretakers are valuable, they can never replace the bond between a parent and their child. Your attention and care are more impactful than you realize. A lot can go wrong

ENDLESS QUEST

when you're absent; use my experiences as a guide to do better. Together, we can break the cycle and restore the families God intended us to have.

FOREWORD

In a world where family structures are evolving and becoming increasingly diverse, the conversation about single parenting has never been more relevant. This book delves into the profound and multifaceted effects of single parenting on children, uncovering the unique challenges and triumphs experienced by parents and children within this dynamic family structure.

Blending research, biblical wisdom, and personal stories, this book helps readers understand how scriptural principles can be applied practically to single parenting. It offers hope and insight into the redemption and growth of children raised in one-parent households. Through this journey, readers are invited to explore the transformative power of faith and its ability to shape and strengthen single-parent families.

As we examine the complexities of modern family life, it is crucial to acknowledge the distinct journeys of children growing up in single-parent homes. These children may face significant challenges that impact their development, but they also demonstrate remarkable resilience, adaptability, and emotional depth. Through research-backed insights and heartfelt narratives, this book sheds light on their emotional and psychological experiences, celebrating their strength and potential.

The author weaves knowledge from personal experience, biblical teachings, interviews, and case studies. Rather than viewing single parent living as a challenge to overcome, this book redefines it as a unique and empowering family structure that deserves understanding, compassion, and unwavering support.

As you navigate these chapters, I encourage you to reflect on the lessons shared, whether you are a single parent or someone seeking to support and uplift families in this context. This book explores the trials of single parenting and celebrates resilience, redemption, and hope that emerge through faith and perseverance.

Let us recognize the profound impact single parenting has on children and the extraordinary potential that exists within every child, regardless of their family configuration. Together, we can foster a deeper appreciation for families' diverse paths and celebrate their unique strengths and victories.

It is an honor to write this foreword. As a mother, a woman of faith, a nurse for over two decades, and an educator, I resonate deeply with the themes of this book. Raised by an emotionally absent father, I have experienced the realities of the challenges it explores. Similarly, my daughter, whom I raised alone, grew up without the love and support of a consistently present father. Today, she is happily married, a testament to the resilience and grace that God bestows. I see God's hand in Vivienne's life and her gift for writing. I pray this book touches your heart as profoundly as it has touched mine.

Evelin Viera, MSN, RN, CCM

ACKNOWLEDGMENTS

First and foremost, I want to thank God for His unfailing faithfulness and grace throughout my life. His kindness and mercy have been my constant companions. Without His guidance, healing, and strength, this book would not have been possible.

To my mother: You are, without question, the strongest woman I know. People may call me strong, but the truth is, Momma, you're the source of that strength. Your resilience, sacrifice, and unwavering love have shaped me into who I am today. Your provision and protection were immeasurable, and this book is as much your story as it is mine. I am forever grateful for the countless ways you showed up for me, even when the world's weight rested on your shoulders. You're phenomenal, and I love you endlessly.

To my big sister: We have shared this life for as long as I can remember, and despite the many challenges, the Lord has been our protector and warrior. Because of Him, we've come out stronger. Growing up, I'll admit there were times I wished I could trade you for someone else, but life has taught me that there is no one else I'd rather have by my side. Let us continue creating more joyful memories together. I love you, and I'm thankful for the bond we share.

To my future husband and children: This book is my release from the past. I once delayed writing it, thinking I needed to be married first, but now I see the importance of obeying God's call in His time. This book shows my healing, forgiveness, and preparation for a brighter future with you. It reflects my commitment to grow and be the best version of myself for our family. Thank you in advance for being my anchor, motivation, and reason to keep pushing forward. Your love, understanding, and encouragement inspire me even before we meet, and I can't wait to share this journey of life and love with you.

To my grandma: You were the angel God sent to us in our time of need. Thank you for opening your home and heart to us and giving my mom the chance to raise us under your care. Every day, you worked tirelessly to ensure we were safe, fed, and prepared for life. I'll never forget how, without fail, lunch was always ready at 1 p.m. when I came home from school. Your discipline and promptness taught me the value of time, a lesson I carry with me today. I love and appreciate you more than words can express. May the Lord keep you; yes, those great-grandchildren are coming soon! Hahaha.

To all the men and women of God who have held my hand over the years: You are incredible! I am deeply grateful for my pastors, teachers, mentors, and colleagues in the work of the Lord. The church at All People in North Reading, Massachusetts, has been my home, healing place, and safe space. Thank you for being an integral part of my journey.

To everyone who has played a part in my life: relatives, friends, and my mom's friends, thank you for your unwavering support, prayers, and belief in me. Your words of encouragement sustained me through my toughest moments. To my friends who generously shared their personal stories and experiences of upbringing with me, your openness has been a gift. Each story is a treasure that has expanded my perspective and helped me connect to life beyond my experiences.

To Ms. Evelin Viera: Your foreword is a blessing, and I am so grateful for your friendship. Thank you for your love, kindness, and willingness to be used by God. Your words and presence are a constant source of joy and encouragement. Thank you for reading this book and sharing your story as a single mother on my show at Photizo Daily. Your authenticity and faith inspire me, and I am excited for the work God will continue to do through us to impact the world. Amen!

Lastly, to my late father: I am deeply thankful to God for allowing me the opportunity to pursue a relationship with you. Learning that your presence in my life was not just a want, but a need was one of the most humbling and transformative realizations I have ever had. If I had known earlier how your absence would leave such a void in my heart and shape so much of my journey, I would have fought harder to keep you in my life. I would have let go of my pride and pain, forgiven sooner, and never blocked you out. Yet, I have learned strength, independence, and determination. This book reflects my growth, healing, and commitment to breaking the cycle for future generations. This is not just my story; this is our legacy.

INTRODUCTION

My sister and I began living with our mom in high school. Despite the challenges of being a single mother, she worked tirelessly to ensure we attended boarding school, a privilege I grew to appreciate deeply. When I returned home from school that holiday, I was surprised to see boys sitting at our shop. This was the first time for my mom, who had always been so strict about us interacting with men.

She never allowed us to talk to any man for anything other than business at the shop, and they had to leave immediately after they were done. But with these boys, she let them stay for hours. Over time, I learned that these boys were pastor's kids, and soon, they invited us to their church. Gradually, we formed friendships that I cherish to this day, although they are no longer as strong. Living with our mom brought more friction than the peaceful days we spent with our grandmother during primary school. Still, I cherished being with her, especially because of the support, great conversations, and camaraderie shared with these friends.

One brought me a book after learning about my love for reading. If I remember correctly, the book was titled Love, Sex, and Relationships. Though much of the book has faded from memory, one statement stood out: ***"If a girl has not had her dad present growing up, she gives herself to men."*** As a teenager without a present father, those words felt like a slap in the face. I could not believe, let alone accept, such a statement. The idea of "giving myself to men" was so repellent that I stopped reading the book. I did not discuss or challenge it; I just let it go.

My mom, ever protective, kept a close watch over us. She shielded us from the men who often showed up at our shop, likely trying to catch our attention. But even with her vigilance, I knew the decision was ultimately mine. I resolved never to give myself to men or engage in the sneaky behavior I often saw among girls my age. I promised myself I'd never be caught in compromising situations, no sneaking around, and no hidden conversations. If I spoke to boys, everything felt safe and transparent in our shop or church. Attending a same-sex school further reinforced my distance from boys, making it easier to maintain my resolve.

Looking back, I realize I misunderstood that statement from the book. At the time, I was defensive, interpreting it as a judgment rather than an observation. As I have grown and encountered life's complexities, I now see that the statement was not entirely wrong but simply incomplete. It spoke to a truth about the emotional void left by an absent father, which manifests differently for everyone.

CHAPTER ONE

THE UNSEEN DAD

"My father did not tell me how to live; he lived and let me watch him do it."
–Clarence Budington Kelland

Growing up in a conservative family and culture, it was normal for children not to ask certain questions. Today, children are free to inquire about anything, especially in some parts of the world. But where I was raised, that was unthinkable. Asking certain questions was often viewed as disrespectful, and parents could take offence.

While this approach is usually rooted in a desire to protect children's innocence, it leaves an emotional burden that many carry for years. When parents avoid addressing important truths or events within the family, they leave children with unanswered questions and pieces of their past they are left to wonder about, sometimes for a lifetime.

Growing Up Without a Dad

Questions like why one parent is no longer home, why we stopped visiting certain places or people, why someone no longer comes around, or why we are moving are often unexplained. Many parents think keeping children in the dark shields them from pain, but it can create confusion and unspoken hurt instead. The truth has the power to free us.

When we are open to our children about the realities of life, especially those that directly affect them, we relieve them of the emotional weight of wondering all their lives. Just because children do not express their thoughts does not mean they aren't troubled by them. Their silence does not equal peace.

Reflecting on my upbringing, I have grown to appreciate the openness of certain cultures, particularly Western cultures, where children are often included in important family discussions and decisions. In my experience, it was not like that. No one asked for my opinion or even how I felt about things, and besides, there weren't many options to choose from anyway. hahaha.

Decisions were made for us, from what we ate to where we went, and we accepted them without question. Above all, there was so much to be grateful for. There was always food, shelter, school fees, and clothes. What more could a child ask for when their mother was working tirelessly to provide?

As I have grown, I have realized that children need more than just their physical needs met. Emotional and psychological needs are just as important, and when they go unaddressed, they can leave deep and lasting scars. These needs often arise from what children see, hear, and think, things they may not know how to articulate but feel deeply. It can profoundly affect them when they can't express these feelings or ask questions that weigh on their hearts.

Too often, we assume that providing for a child's physical needs is enough. But the emotional weight of silence or unanswered questions can be just as damaging, if not more so. Children need to feel seen, heard, validated, and not just cared for physically.

Without this, the emotional void left behind can carry consequences that linger well into adulthood.

Life in Kyabazaala Village

The obscure story I have been told is that when I was just 9 months old, I was taken to my great-grandmother's village in Kyabazaala, Kayunga District, Uganda. I do not know every detail of why this happened, but from what my mom has shared in recent years, I have pieced together that it stemmed from a toxic relationship between my parents. I later learned that their separation was far from amicable. My dad did not want my mom to leave, but she was determined and hoped our dad would not see us until we were 20.

    I grew up in that village, creating countless memories, some of which I still cherish and would love to share with you. I remember always being carried on my great-grandmother's back. She tried to trick me into drinking porridge mixed with milk, knowing how much I loved porridge, but I hated milk. Even as a little child, I did not fall for it; I have never taken milk to this day!

    I remember going to the garden, cooking over firewood, fetching water from the well after school, and playing outside until sunset. At night, we were often too scared to bathe because our grandmothers would tell us stories about "night dancers" (cannibals) who might come for us. We climbed trees to pick avocados, mangoes, pawpaws (papaya), and jackfruit, savoring the rewards of our little adventures.

    Chores were part of life, even for children. I vividly remember digging around the house before school, a task I despised back then but have come to appreciate as an adult. It taught me a skill and the value of hard work. Life is full of chores anyway, so I'm glad I started learning early. I also remember when I was supposed to move up to a new class, but I cried so much because I did not want to leave the familiarity of my old one. The teachers, unable to console me, let me repeat the year. Thinking back now, it makes me laugh!

My mom visited us often, and those days were special. She would bring fried chicken, French fries (what we call chips in Uganda), and snacks for our school break and lunch boxes. Though she hoped the food would last for some time, it rarely did; our great-grandmother would generously share most of it with relatives and neighbors. Everyone in the village looked forward to my mom's visits. It was as exciting as a visiting day at boarding school, filled with anticipation and joy.

Not every memory was sweet, though. There were tough seasons when we did not have sauce (enva) to make a complete meal. On those days, we would cook matooke (green bananas) and use salty water as our sauce. I still laugh when I think about one evening when my grandmother bought silverfish from the market, a rare treat in that season. We were so excited about the meal, but it was my sister's turn to cook, and as she carried the saucepan from the kitchen, a strong wind blew. Terrified that a "night dancer" was near, she ran off, dropping the entire saucepan. All our precious silverfish spilled onto the ground. What a disappointment after we had been salivating at the thought of a delicious meal!

Other memories bring a mix of humor and insecurity. I cried so much whenever I had to lose a tooth that my great-grandmother eventually decided not to force me. As a result, my teeth did not grow properly, which became a big insecurity as I got older. To this day, I'm obsessed with people's teeth because those childhood memories still linger.

Our childhood was not filled with TV shows like many others remember. We did not have a television and did not miss it because we were too busy playing outside and climbing trees. Sometimes, I'd get stuck in a tree, crying for help, while no one knew where I was! I only became aware of TV when we walked miles to watch the royal wedding of the Kabaka (King of Buganda). My grandma told us days in advance that we would go to the wedding, and I genuinely thought we were attending the event in person. On the big day, we showered and dressed in our finest clothes, only to realize we were walking to a relative's house miles away to watch it on TV. What a surprise! I had expected a grand party, hahaha.

Fear and Absence of a Father Figure

Among all these memories, one saying from my childhood echoes loudest: *"When you see a big, tall man, run."* To this day, I do not know who told us that, but as children, we believed it wholeheartedly. We were told that our dad was a tall, big man trying to find us, and fear was instilled in us. It didn't bother me because I had never seen or known anything like a dad. Whenever I saw a tall man, whether at the well, in the garden, or on the road, I would run. To me, all men were kidnappers, hahaha. Because of this fear, I never learned the vocabulary of "daddy" or "dad. Those words felt foreign to me as we grew, and in my world, "parent" meant "mother." My mom visited us, and my grandmothers oversaw everything else.

Looking back, I see the gaps in my understanding as a child and the emotional impact of not having a father present. These experiences shaped me in ways I did not fully grasp then. Yet, they also taught me resilience, gratitude, and the value of family, even in its imperfect forms. The absence of a father does not simply vanish as a child grows older; instead, it lingers like a shadow, coloring experiences and shaping how we perceive relationships.

> *"Fatherhood is the ultimate responsibility of a man. The destiny of nations rests on the shoulders of fathers."*
> *– Dr. Myles Munroe.*

CHAPTER TWO

TRACING SHADOWS

> *"I realize I'm constantly searching for guys to fill that void in me. I do not want a relationship; I want a father. I had never realized how much my father's absence hurt until I stopped shoving it far into the back of my mind."*
>
> *- Unknown.*

Learning About a Father for the First Time

When I started school, I learned that there was such a thing as a father in every family, which made me wonder what had happened to mine. I then remembered the warning we had been given before about the big, tall man. From then on, I could not help but think, **"Where is My Dad At?"** I loved watching the sunset in our quiet neighborhood, its long shadows becoming a canvas for my thoughts. Even now, sunsets fascinate me. As a child, I often climbed trees and sat there, lost in my musings about the tall, big man whose absence had started looming over me like a shadow.

Although I did not know him, his absence became a constant presence. I often imagined what it would feel like to know him, but I never spoke about these thoughts to anyone. The idea of a father was not part of our daily lives; no one mentioned him. My world revolved around my mother, grandmother, and great-grandmother, yet I always wondered who he was.

We lived in the village until I was about seven years old. At one point, my sister and I became so sick that my mom brought us back to the city of Kampala for treatment. She recalls how, even with painful sores in our mouths, we still managed to eat the fried chicken she had made. Watching us eat despite the pain, she decided not to return us to the village.

For a short while, we stayed with her before moving to her mother's house, as my mom needed to work and could not care for us full-time. She visited us every Sunday without fail, bringing whatever she had for the week. Growing up with our cousins, I made countless memories there, including falling from a neighbor's tree and spraining my right wrist during our early days there, hahaha, and every evening, my grandma had to use ghee to massage my sprained hand. I hated it because it was painful, but it brought relief.

Meeting my Dad for the First Time

When I was eleven, a woman I did not recognize approached us while we played in the neighborhood. She asked if we knew "Jjaaja Derrick," meaning Derrick's grandmother, which name our grandma was commonly called. I did not ask who she was; I took her to meet my grandma. To my surprise, my grandma was delighted to see her. She turned out to be my dad's mother, my paternal grandmother!

That moment filled me with joy, not because I fully understood what it meant, but because it ignited dreams of finally meeting the tall, big man I had imagined for so long. My paternal grandmother had heard from a construction worker in her neighborhood that my dad resembled some children he had seen. After gathering more information, she decided to find us. Though my mom had wanted to keep us away from our dad until we were older, her mother did not follow this plan. Both grandmothers stayed in touch and eventually agreed that we would meet our dad. I do not remember exactly how I felt when I first saw him, but I do remember that he fit the image I had held of him: tall and big, just as I had imagined.

Unmet Expectations and Growing Disappointment

Meeting my dad filled me with hope. I thought he would do all the things my mom could not. For instance, my mom, a tailor, only purchased the school uniforms once when we first joined the school and decided to make them herself as we grew, but the colors never matched the official shade of yellow. This was annoying and embarrassing to me. It made me dread school, though I had no choice but to go. When I met my dad, I hoped he would change things like this. I thought all my prayers and dreams would finally come true...hahaha.

But reality fell short of my expectations. One holiday, while staying at my paternal grandmother's house, I wrote a school shopping list for my dad, just as we always did for my mom. When he saw the list, he said, "I, Robert, can't afford this. Only your mom can do this; Zalwango is rich." I was shocked! The tall, big man with a wallet in his shirt pocket said he did not have money. This was the first time I heard a man say he did not have money. I used to think men, especially those with sizable bellies, always had money, hahaha! My heart sank. He could not understand why we did not attend a day school, which he found more affordable. That moment broke something in me.

Though my mom was unhappy that my grandma had taken us to meet our dad, she later admitted it helped us know and understand who he was. He started visiting during the holidays, and while he occasionally bought me small things I asked for, he never met the expectations I had placed on him. These unmet expectations created a growing gap between us that later felt impossible to bridge.

One vivid memory is of a parent-teacher meeting at school. My mom could not attend, so she asked my dad to go. He arrived, but all he brought were newspapers. I was stunned and angry. My mom never came to school without bringing food or other essentials for boarding school life. Yet, looking at him that day, something shifted in me. I realized, "Whether you like it or not, he is still your dad." I saw myself in him as though looking in a mirror.

Lessons from a Complicated Father-Daughter Relationship

Over time, I discovered that my dad had another family. This made me believe that he left us for them because he did not love us, which is why he refused to fulfill my requests. After growing up and taking up my financial responsibilities, I began to understand some of the challenges my dad might have faced. Supporting two families without a stable income as a businessman and shop owner could have been difficult. While it does not excuse everything, it helps me see why he struggled to provide consistently. He easily overlooked whether we had food or other necessities because he had no relationship with us. I have learned that two parents are always better than one because they get to share the emotional and financial burdens of raising children.

Looking back, I wish my mom, or even our dad, had told us earlier why he could not meet my expectations. I never asked, but that did not mean I wasn't thinking about it. Children may be young, but they are never too young to grasp what affects or concerns them. Because I couldn't understand, I believed he didn't love us. Later, as an adult, my mum shared how, over the years, she had often wondered what happened to my dad. Despite their issues, he had always been a devoted father when they were still together, coming home early, bathing my big sister, cooking, washing clothes, fetching water, and proudly walking everywhere with her.

After they separated, everything changed; he did not seem to care anymore in our absence. In our culture, parents often avoid explaining their struggles to children, leaving them to interpret silence as rejection. For years, I believed my dad did not love us. I felt abandoned. He likely had his reasons, reasons I'll never fully understand.

However, I am deeply grateful to my late great grandma (RIP) and her family in the village, who took care of me from when I was a baby. I am indebted to my maternal grandmother for her sacrifices, including quitting her job to stay home and care for us. I'm so thankful to all my mum's friends who have supported her relentlessly throughout the years. God bless you for your kindness! I'm also thankful to God for my uncles, especially my favorite uncle, the late Uncle Peter, who always bought me stylish clothes and accessories my mom refused to get for me or could not afford. May his soul rest in peace. My bonus uncle, Uncle Ssuubi, always tirelessly helped us. God bless you, sir! I am thankful for my dad's siblings, especially Uncle Fred, who I remember coming through financially whenever he could through college.

My paternal grandmother was a gem; she always gave me whatever she had whenever I showed up at her house. Her home became my safe space during university, where I could rest and recharge. She showed me the power of generosity, a value I have carried into my life. May her dear soul rest in peace. Despite having all this support, nobody ever explained or said anything about how our dad related to us.

Through all this, I have learned the importance of close and extended family, which many of us today, especially immigrants, don't have closely and presently. I appreciate the need for meaningful relationships and communication between parents and children. Without open communication, children can feel unloved, leading to deep insecurities. Parents must become a safe space for their children, encouraging them to express their thoughts and emotions freely. Words matter; harsh or dismissive statements can leave lasting scars, while intentional, loving words can build confidence and trust. Words either build or break.

Time and again, I often wish I had a relationship with my dad. Though I am a lot like my mom, there are qualities my mom says I inherited from my dad, which could have been nurtured further if he had been present. I find myself seeking male mentors to fill the gap, but I still wish my dad had been my constant. Seeing fathers with their children always brings a pang of longing. It is a reminder of what could have been.

I have often asked a close friend to adopt me because I deeply admire the kind of dad he is to his two daughters. I like to see dads proud of their kids, and I love listening and watching them. The first thing I notice about any man is whether he seems like a good father. This has shaped my relationships, as I have struggled to trust that someone could be the kind of father I want for my future children. I know this longing will always be a part of me, an echo of the little girl who wished for her dad to be present.

Road to Adulthood
As teenagers, we had constant conflict with our mom. Her attempts to exercise parental authority often felt overbearing and dominant. While she was physically present, our relationship lacked the openness where I could comfortably express myself. I did not feel free to share my thoughts or feelings whenever I wanted. I vividly remember one incident when she withdrew the phone; we used to communicate with her while staying at our paternal grandma's house.

Frustrated, I asked if I could use her phone to call a friend, but she refused. Feeling unheard, I wrote her a letter, pouring out my feelings for the first time. Little did I know I was getting into more trouble! Soon, my uncle called and talked to me about how "disrespectful" I was. What? What wrong had I done? Are parents always, right? Feel free to share your answers, hahaha.

Looking back, I realize that most of what my mom did came from a place of protection. However, I also know that children need more than one parent for balanced emotional development. When one parent disciplines, the other can provide comfort. What happens, though, when all you have is one parent? There is no balance! If they are dominant, angry, bitter, and unmindful, that is all you have; whatever they are and do, that is it for you, too, as a child. And for us, whatever our mom was, it was all we had, even when we didn't appreciate it.

Despite the frequent clashes, I was a compliant child. My mom did not have many issues with me, though I often struggled internally. I was always upset but was not as openly defiant as my sister. hahaha. Quietly, I looked forward to adulthood, imagining the day I could leave her space and make my own decisions. I longed for the freedom to attend church activities without restrictions, to escape her calculated curfews. Our family friends, boys and girls, seemed to enjoy much more freedom than we did. They could attend all the church events they wanted, but being home even a minute past the set time was unimaginable for us. I hated it! Even the church had limits. I hated it!

Music and books became my closest companions, offering solace during those turbulent years. One day, I confided in the friend who had given me that book years ago, sharing how unfair I thought my mom was. He had witnessed some of her strictness firsthand, so I expected him to validate my feelings. But instead, he said, **"Vivienne, just be calm."**

Those words weren't what I wanted to hear. I wanted him to tell me he understood and explain why my mom was so tough. But today, I can say they were exactly what I needed. From that moment on, I decided to stay calm, no matter what my mom did. It was not easy, but it changed everything. That simple advice turned out to be the best I have ever received.

My journey to adulthood has been complex and transformative, and, like many others, I have never felt fully ready for it. Sometimes, I wish I had been better prepared. It was not until I became an adult, far away from my family, that I realized having my dad present was not just something I wanted; it was something I needed. The absence I had felt as a child became even more apparent as I navigated the challenges of adulthood.

While my childhood was filled with unanswered questions about my father, adolescence brought its own set of challenges. Emotional gaps began to manifest in ways I could not yet comprehend. Relationships, friendships, and unspoken fears began to surface, revealing just how deeply the absence of a father can impact a child's sense of worth and belonging.

> *"The most important thing you will leave behind is not your possessions but the legacy of godly fatherhood you've imparted to your children."*
>
> *– Mark Driscoll.*

CHAPTER THREE

BROKEN EARLY

"The father who does not teach his son his duties is equally guilty with the son who neglects them."
– Adrian Rogers.

The Pain of Rejection

Growing up without a relationship with my dad made it easy for me to cut him off once I realized he would not meet my expectations or help me understand why he could not. It was easy to live without him, to act as though I did not have a dad, and even easier to forget he existed, at least on the surface. The few times I tried to engage with him only led to disappointment and conflict because of his inability to meet my needs.

One instance stands out clearly in my memory. My mom had traveled to the village for her father's burial, leaving me at home with my baby cousin. We ran out of money, so I called my dad for help. His response was the same: he did not have money. Hearing this yet again broke me. Whether it was true or not, it did not matter. I heard rejection loud and clear. I was tired of asking, tired of being let down. That day, I blocked him. He was the first person I ever blocked in my life. hahaha.

Over the years, I adapted to life without him. I told myself I did not need him. But even though I learned to function without his presence, I could not erase the fact that he existed. There were moments, especially during my university years when I felt his absence acutely.

Times of lack reminded me of the father I wished I had. My mom was doing her best, but there was still so much need. I remember one day at university, feeling particularly hungry and wanting to treat myself to something special. I decided to call the "main man," hoping things might be different this time. But, as usual, he said he could not help. It crushed me.

Moments like these opened deeper voids in my heart. The endless wishes and unmet longings created a yearning for fulfillment, sometimes in ways that could have led me down the wrong path. It was during this time that I began to understand why some girls my age turned to multiple boyfriends or sought validation in unhealthy relationships. The absence of a father figure leaves a gap that many, including myself, instinctively sought to fill, unaware.

Searching for Fulfillment

In those days, I felt an undeniable pull toward men. I started reconnecting with former teachers who had been kind to me, people I had met during internships, lecturers, and others who seemed approachable. I was not just looking for financial support; I craved guidance, inspiration, mentorship, and someone who would listen to and understand me. Even today, I remain deeply fascinated by men who truly take the time to listen. For those who did, I'm incredibly thankful.

But not all these encounters turned out well. While I saw many of these men as mentors and father figures, not all of them saw me the same way. Some viewed me as more than a friend, student, or daughter; they saw an opportunity to gratify their desires. These experiences left me frustrated and extremely disappointed. By the time I graduated and landed my first job, I was thoroughly disillusioned with many men I had once looked up to.

Yet not all was lost. I am immensely grateful for the good friends and church community that gave me company and solace. I thank God for finding me early when I joined the university. Looking back, I can see His hand guiding me and surrounding me with people who mentored me toward a life of intentional faith. Though my journey has been imperfect, my life could have taken a far darker turn if God hadn't intervened.

Though initially hesitant, the fellowships I joined at university became a lifeline. They placed me in circles with other young people on similar journeys, seeking to know God and build their identity in Him. While others got lost in drunkenness, addictions, and reckless partying, succumbing to the challenges of peer pressure and young adulthood, I was being pulled toward something greater. These people encouraged me to find my worth in God rather than what I lacked or the approval I sought from others.

This is my biggest testimony: I never would have made it without God. His grace and the people He brought into my life saved me at college, redirecting my steps when I was on the verge of losing my way. For that, I will always be thankful.

Carving My Horn Through Friendships: Friendships That Shaped Me

Although I attended a same-sex high school, I have always found it easier to form friendships with men than with women. I often gravitate toward male friends and build connections with older, wiser, driven, kind, and more accomplished people who inspire me or lead in significant ways. I do not form many associations with my peers; the few I do are with individuals who stand out as exceptionally wise or skilled in something that draws me to them. Typically, the only people younger than me in my circle are those I mentor and inspire.

As I transitioned from my late teens to my early 20s, I realized I needed more support than my mom could provide, not just financially. I needed emotional support, and with so many questions about different things in my life, I could never ask her because I didn't learn to be free with her; I didn't learn to ask whatever I was thinking. Thankfully, God took hold of my heart profoundly and personally during this pivotal time. While I had been born again before, it was not until I started university that I truly experienced Him for myself. Though I didn't know much, I could tell He was holding me up by His grace.

There became a deep vacuum in my life that I had been trying to fill, though I did not fully understand what I needed. Despite making many friends, not all of them were genuine. Some friendships turned into bitter disappointments, especially with men I had respected as father figures, uncles, or brothers, only to discover their intentions were far from what I had thought.

Fighting My Way Through

"Boundaries are for protection"
-Pastor Stephanie Ike

Nothing has always frustrated me more than a man who claims to love his daughter and dreams of the best for her yet manipulates other people's daughters. I recall one particularly disheartening experience during my job search. I was introduced to a seemingly respectable man who promised to connect me with someone who had job leads. Instead, I later realized that both men had ulterior motives. This is appalling yet so common, many men manipulate young girls.

They used kind words and false promises, preying on my naivety and manipulating me into their circle. I thought they saw me as a daughter and were helping me out of goodwill. One day, one of them boldly confessed his feelings for me after telling me about his beloved daughter. I was shocked and disgusted. All I could think was, ***"Do you think I was not born with dreams? Do you think I do not have a future where you'd ask me to compromise my life for you?"***

For the first time, I spoke up; I was so tired! This experience and others like it made me lose respect for certain people, even some who knew my mom. It is heartbreaking to see such hypocrisy: men who want the best for their children yet manipulate other people's children. It is greatly upsetting and an indictment of their character. Neglecting or failing to guide your children leaves them vulnerable to the world as prey to reckless and shameless people. Sadly, this is the reality for many.

Though I am thankful for the kindness I have received from many people, only a few friendships were genuine. I do not want anyone, especially young people, to go through the struggles and confusion I faced in navigating relationships and friendships with men without understanding how to set boundaries. That's why I'm sharing this. When parents do not engage their children in these matters, they leave them vulnerable to manipulation, abuse, and toxic influences. The devil is always lurking, looking for opportunities to exploit idle or unaware children.

Parents, I urge you to teach your children, especially your daughters, how to recognize and set boundaries in friendships and relationships. Be vigilant about who befriends them, particularly men who lack moral and spiritual grounding. The devil does not come dressed as the enemy, hahaha. He often disguises himself, slipping into the lives of those who are unprepared. No one taught me this; I had to learn through painful experiences. But I hope that by sharing my story, someone else can avoid the same mistakes and find protection in wisdom, guidance, and God's grace.

Amid the emotional struggles of growing up without a father, I began to seek answers and guidance in unexpected places. While my dad was not present to meet my needs, God began placing spiritual mentors in my life who, for a long time, helped fill some gaps. Through their wisdom and leadership, these men became vessels of God's love, teaching me to trust God and grow in my purpose.

> *"The way you treat your children teaches them how to treat others. A father's example is the most important thing a child will ever have."*
> – Rick Warren.

CHAPTER FOUR

THROUGH SPIRITUAL FATHERS

"Being a father means taking responsibility for your child's spiritual, emotional, and physical well-being."
– *Bishop T.D. Jakes*

Struggling to Relate to God as a Father

Growing up without a father figure, I never experienced strict authority from any man or the need to give accountability to any man. When these dynamics eventually entered my life, I struggled to process them. In Christian fellowships at college, people often asked who my spiritual father was, and I had no answer. I couldn't imagine having anyone as my father! I was still figuring out my salvation journey. Although I had accepted Jesus Christ early in my primary school years and repeatedly during altar calls, I hadn't taken my salvation seriously.

The phrase "God is a Father" did not resonate with me because the word "father" held little meaning in my life. I believed in Jesus but did not want anything about his father being a father to me, too. At the same time, I loved and lived for secular music. It brought me so much pleasure. Every sermon I heard emphasized God as a father, and that I could not love both God and secular music, and since I did not understand the "God the Father" concept, the music felt more relatable and fulfilling to me.

However, my priorities shifted as I gradually developed my understanding of God and His love at the university. I began to find deeper joy in studying His Word, spending time in His presence, and engaging in ministry. Letting go of secular music was initially a struggle; it had become an addiction for me. Music, being spiritual, had a hold on me. But as I hungered more for God, the desire for secular music faded effortlessly. Today, I still love music, but it no longer controls me as it once did.

Finding, Comfort, and Inspiration in Church

During this period of spiritual growth, I strongly desired a spiritual father to whom I could identify and be accountable. Though I had been loved and mentored by many, I longed for a deeper level of accountability and connection. God, in His kindness, brought me to learn of some amazing men of God who became so instrumental in my life through their teachings. Apostle Isaiah Ainebyoona and Apostle Grace Lubega have continued to inspire me greatly over the years, also being some of the humblest people I have known.

I grew a strong yearning for sincere and meaningful relationships, I wanted to belong. I found this within the church, stemming from the absence of strong bonds in my upbringing. Raised by my grandmother, alongside my sister and cousin, my mother's weekly Sunday visits did not foster deep family connections. My mom provided everything we needed and cared deeply about our success, especially in school. Knowing that a good class report was important to her, I always delivered. But beyond meeting her expectations, I struggled with low self-esteem and found it difficult to build meaningful relationships with others. People who knew me in the past can attest to how shy and reserved I was, though many refuse to believe it now...hahaha.

Reflecting on this, I have realized how much our upbringing shapes how we relate to others later in life. Music became a refuge because it allowed me to be alone. It did not require human interaction and brought satisfaction without the complexities of relationships. While church eventually opened me up to people, solitude remained my comfort zone. Do not get me wrong; I love being around authentic people.

University was a transformative period for me. It rooted me in the church and taught me how to navigate some relationships. I felt my life's voids slowly filling through serving, submitting, and being accountable in church. I grew to honor and love men of God so deeply that I completely stopped thinking my biological father was necessary for my life. On Father's Day, for many years, I only celebrated my mom, spiritual father, and mentors, completely forgetting about my biological dad.

This part of my story is deeply personal because I understand how the church can become a refuge and even a family for many of us. In my experience, I found comfort and support through pastors, instructors, and my spiritual father. Nevertheless, as I grew, I began to realize that no one could replace my biological father if he were alive. Even as I served and loved in church, there was a lingering feeling that something was missing.

People often thought I was overly independent, intimidating, or even tough. One person I dated called me a bully, while others said I was too principled, serious, or spiritual. On the other hand, I thought they were disrespectful, did not know how to treat me, or did not listen. But looking back, I see the real issue: I had no model for what to expect from men or how to treat them.

Where had I learned how to navigate relationships with men? Nowhere.

Despite studying and applying myself to understanding relationships, I found it difficult even to trust my choices. I did not feel loved or respected, no matter how much I tried. I could tell something was lacking. I realized I needed a personal relationship with at least a father figure to help me understand and navigate this journey. For years, I had dismissed the idea of reconnecting with my dad, thinking it was not worth pursuing, especially because he hadn't sought me out.

Choosing Reconciliation over Resentment

But then came one Sunday in December 2018. One pastor in a church I had been attending in that season, Pastor Fredrick, preached a sermon on forgiveness and reconciliation, specifically addressing parent-child relationships. He emphasized that regardless of the past, we must forgive and make peace with our parents. The message felt deeply personal. I hadn't spoken to my dad in over a year and had my reasons, but the Holy Spirit prompted me to reach out.

A month later, I did. My dad was glad to hear from me, and I decided to pursue a relationship with him not out of emotion but out of obedience to God. Though our relationship remained bumpy, I was intentional about showing up for him, even in ways he hadn't been able to show up for me. Sharing devotionals and teachings with him became a new way of connecting, and he blessed me every time I reached out. Though I did it reluctantly, these small moments mattered, and they still do. They remind me of the peace that comes with obeying God. I chose peace. And in that peace, I found healing.

The Missing Blueprint of Love

As I have grown, I have understood how profoundly fathers shape a girl's understanding of love and relationships. A father's love sets the blueprint for healthy, respectful connections. Without that foundation, navigating relationships can feel like walking in the dark without a map. If I were to write another book, it would be about the countless challenges I have faced in this area, rooted in the absence of my father's guidance.

While many people see me as strong, smart, or even proud, few realize the internal battles I have endured. Struggles do not disappear because of principles or just caution. Despite being intentional and guarded in my approach, I have often found myself unsure: How much attention should I expect? What treatment is acceptable? How much should I endure?

Growing up, my mom was the only authority figure I fully answered to. Her dominance shaped my view of authority, and as a teenager, I could not wait to turn 18 and find some breathing room. When men later tried to exercise authority over me without explanation, like my mom, it triggered something in me. It often felt like dictatorship rather than leadership, and I did not know how much to tolerate. It brought out the worst in me. Relationships during this period were marked by patience, confusion, and eventual frustration.

Looking back, I realize the issue was not my resistance to authority but the kind of authority I encountered. In His grace, God has taught me through new experiences that I do not hate authority but dislike being controlled. What I need is a servant leader, someone who communicates and collaborates rather than dictates. At the same time, I have learned that I also cannot follow someone who cannot or refuses to lead. The root issue of settling for less was that I was not self-aware and had no clear model of what I was trying to build. Without an image or shadow to reflect on, my love journey felt blurry and undefined.

This lack of a father figure affects not just romantic relationships but every facet of self-worth and interpersonal dynamics. It has been a process of trial and error, filled with lessons learned through pain and guidance sought from mentors, friends, and, most importantly, God, who graciously embraced me even when I sought Him as a last resort, reminding me that He should always be my first resort.

Relationships

During my university years, while many around me found relationships that led to marriage, I chose a different path. I let go of a budding relationship because it conflicted with my pursuit of God. Instead, I dedicated myself to ministry, my studies, and nurturing friendships with people I still hold dear, those we fondly called "papas" and "mamas." As my zeal for God grew, He brought individuals into my life to mentor, care for, and love unconditionally.

Though I haven't had biological children yet, I have experienced a sense of motherhood through these relationships. I have stayed up late, advised, taught, nurtured, and invested in their growth. Watching God transform their lives has been one of the most fulfilling experiences of my journey. With these fulfilling relationships and a few sermons, I believed I was equipped to navigate a romantic relationship that could lead to marriage. I often prayed for my future husband, even envisioning names for our children.

Unhealthy Love and Misplaced Expectations

When I turned 25, a friend encouraged me to get a boyfriend, but I dismissed the term entirely. I wanted a husband, not just a casual relationship. Just before this time, she had introduced me to someone who immediately turned me off with his overly direct approach. Though he checked on me persistently, I remained uninterested, feeling and knowing he was not as spiritual as I wanted my future husband to be. Yet later, circumstances brought us together occasionally, and I eventually agreed to have lunch with him. During our conversation, he shared his story of losing both parents at a young age.

His vulnerability touched me, and I thought, why not him if I could love and mentor others? Truthfully, I lacked a clear image of the man I desired, yet I knew I wanted to get married. Beyond wanting a tall, fun, and good-looking Christian man, I had no blueprint for what I truly needed in a partner. I was overlooking critical aspects of compatibility. My focus was superficial: his height, hard work, and the fact that he was from my tribe. Though these traits seemed acceptable, even pleasing to my family, we lacked a deeper connection. Our relationship had no solid foundation, shared vision, or understanding of purpose. Even though we appeared to look good together, as many often told us, I continually sensed in my spirit that this relationship was destined for failure.

After one to two months, I felt a strong separation looming, which frightened me, but instead, because I was eager to get married, I ignored my instincts and tried to force love. hahaha. As a proactive person, I began pouring myself into "fixing" him, buying stuff to align him with my preferences, and working hard to make him more lovable in my eyes. Yet, my efforts were in vain. Nothing I did could bridge our spiritual, emotional, and intellectual gaps. There is more to life than what meets the eye. Despite my efforts to make it work, I was often accused of being disrespectful by one who constantly could not lead and protect. Arguments became frequent, especially on Sundays and Tuesdays. Believing the tension stemmed from my secrecy, I decided to tell my mom about the relationship. Her initial reaction was painful; she judged him based on his photo and called him unstable. Hurt, I questioned her judgment, which sparked a significant fight, prompting my sister, who usually stays out of our conflicts, to intervene. Eventually, the storm settled, and he became part of the family, leading us to discuss marriage, but my mum's words lingered.

As the relationship progressed, our incompatibilities became glaring: differing spiritual and intellectual values, poor communication, and a lack of shared interests. After a certain incident that confirmed my mom's instincts and all had dismissed in my spirit for a long time, I eventually ended the relationship. I am about 98.5% convinced that parents, especially mothers, are often right. hahaha. I can't help but wonder, what lessons and insights do you have when you look back on your relationship journeys?

The aftermath of this breakup was devastating. I faced backlash, humiliation, and betrayal, even from friends. Feeling abandoned and unloved, I began to reflect on how much of myself I had given to people outside my family. Without strong familial ties, I had invested everything in friendships and relationships that ultimately failed me, leaving me adrift like an abandoned ship.

Almost a year later, a persistent acquaintance I had dismissed for months suddenly seemed appealing. Despite my reservations, I entered another relationship, hoping he might provide the love I quietly and desperately sought. I had ignored his love messages for months, but we went from 0% to 80% because he was good at it somehow. This surge of emotion was fueled by sheer excitement and idleness during the COVID-19 lockdown. hahaha.

Despite initially sensing that things weren't right, I was determined to make it work. I wanted to be loved; I just wanted to get married. Unfortunately, it soon became clear that he did not genuinely love me; he only loved the idea of having me. While he appeared spiritually grounded, his character soon revealed otherwise.

While we shared some interests, this relationship turned out to be the worst place I could ever travel to and the worst experience of my life: abusive, disrespectful, and toxic. It cost me my sense of self-worth, and I hated the situation and myself, yet I lacked the courage to end it. I knew it was wrong even to entertain the thought of marriage, but fear of starting over and the desire to marry by a certain age kept me tethered to him. I clung to hope and belief until I could no longer hold on.

I was so broken that even when I attended church, tears would flow. Some of those tears we shed in church aren't solely because of the Holy Spirit's touch but a release of the heavy weight of needless pain, grief, and bitterness we often carry. Yet, in all, I would much rather cry in church than in a bar or any destructive place. Church, as always, was my refuge during this painful season. Eventually, I summoned the strength to end the relationship. The decision was agonizing, but I knew I could not continue sacrificing my self-worth for someone who did not value me.

This chapter of my life taught me hard but valuable lessons, yet I know many others who have been through the same. I realized how deeply my lack of a father's influence had shaped my relationships. Without a model for a healthy partnership, I had settled for less than I deserved, mistaking attention and conditional efforts for love. The experience left me fearful of marriage and commitment, and I wondered how others could find harmony in relationships when mine had been so tumultuous.

The lessons I learned in church brought moments of clarity, but life still had a way of pulling me back into reality. The emotional wounds I had carried for so long were not instantly healed, and relationships continued to reveal the deep void left by my father's absence. Coming back to reality meant confronting these struggles head-on, acknowledging where I still needed God's touch to bring true restoration. I learned that it is far from over until you get to the root.

CHAPTER FIVE

BACK TO REALITY

> *"God calls men to be servant leaders in their homes, to sacrifice themselves for their wives and children, and to lead them with love and care."*
>
> – John Piper.

When I was younger, I believed a father's role was to provide, buy things, pay for expenses, or take me places. My desire for his presence was rooted in what he could do for me financially. When he did not meet my expectations, I disregarded him. It even worsened when I began providing for myself. I did not think I could ever need him. This, though I didn't know, opened me to putting and searching for my fatherhood expectations in other people.

Endless Quest for Fathers

Over time, I began to idolize older male friends and later developed a deep admiration and honor for men of God. I held pastors and mentors in high esteem, almost to the point of obsession. I trusted them fully, opening every part of my life to their guidance, validation, and understanding, not knowing I was searching for the father figure I lacked. However, one trusted minister I loved and honored shattered this trust at one point, leaving me hurt and confused about their actions. This betrayal shook my perception of all these people I had loved and trusted with my life and forced me to confront the unrealistic pedestal I had placed them on.

I withdrew into silence, wrestling with my emotions. It was a period of spiritual and relational turmoil. I turned to God, seeking clarity and direction, and soon, He began to reveal the deeper issue: I had been using these men of God to fill a void left by my father. I had set impossible expectations for them, such as expectations of fatherhood and accountability that they were unaware of and never meant to fulfill.

The statement I had read as a teenager, ***"When a girl does not have her father present, she gives herself to men,"*** immediately came back to me after over twelve years; it resonated with me in a way it hadn't before. I saw that my life had been like a plant we studied about in elementary school that would climb anything to find support to grow. I realized that my relationships with mentors, older friends, and even pastors had been an unconscious attempt to find the father I never had.

This revelation brought both clarity and sorrow. I wept at this truth as I sat thinking of the men who had supported me at various times. Some of whom had disappointed me by failing to offer the mentorship and protection I sought. Instead, they sought romantic or inappropriate connections, compounding my hurt. Reflecting on these experiences, I understood they did not owe me fatherhood; I had placed my expectations on the wrong people.

Placement

Through this period of reflection, God also reminded me of the relationships I had withdrawn from, fearing that the men I chose might repeat the patterns I associated with my father. It became clear that broken people often attract other broken people. Like me, many of these men had grown up with absent fathers. They did not know how to treat women respectfully and kindly because no one had taught them. I was angry at this truth, but it also relieved me; it helped me understand why the people I had loved wholeheartedly did not do any better, because nobody was strongly present to teach them to be men.

The absence of parents during formative years leaves a lasting imprint, shaping thoughts, beliefs, and character. I found myself asking, when will this cycle of brokenness end? When will healing begin? The answer whispered in my heart was simple: It starts with us. We can rebuild functional families by sharing our experiences, addressing generational wounds, and prioritizing our children over ego and selfishness. Dysfunction in a family is not God's desire for us; it can be overcome with intentionality, forgiveness, and love. I knew God was up to something!

After this experience of God opening my eyes, I realized I had missed something crucial: a clear standard for the kind of men I allowed into my life. I had no model to emulate, no guiding principles to follow. This realization led me to pursue an intentional relationship with my father, even though I had spent most of my life learning to live without him. No matter how perfect they seemed, I realized no other man could replace him. Our DNA ties us to our parents in ways we can never undo, and there is always a subtle longing to connect with them, whether we admit it or not.

Loss and the Final Blessing

Just as we were beginning to rebuild our relationship, my father passed away suddenly from a heart attack in August 2021. The pain was indescribable. I had waited so long to connect with him, only to lose him when we finally progressed. His final messages to me, "Nsanyuse nyo, Vv" ("I am so happy, Vivienne") and "May God give you what you deserve "are treasures I hold close to my heart. I miss him intensely.

The pain of his loss is not just about missing his presence; it is about grieving the future we could have shared. I had begun to see how our growing relationship could transform my life. For the first time, I felt understood. He answered my questions with pride, and I felt his joy in engaging with me. However, that chapter of my life was abruptly cut short. Still, I am deeply grateful for the chance I had to make peace with myself about my father and, ultimately, with him.

I can't imagine the regret I would feel if I had only realized the importance of this after he was already gone. If you ever have the chance to make peace, please take it, as tomorrow is never guaranteed. There are so many questions I still wish I could have asked him, especially now as I prepare for marriage. I often wonder 'about the kind of man he wanted for me and the wisdom he could have shared. Losing him has taught me that having a father is not just a longing but a profound and irreplaceable need. ***I miss you, Taata.***

It Is Not a Want – The Irreplaceable Role of a Father

One of this book's purposes is to awaken and remind readers and bring awareness to an issue I believe is often overlooked and dismissed: the commonly underrated yet profound need for fathers and the weight of becoming a parent without truly counting the cost. In today's world, many young people step into parenthood without understanding its responsibilities. While these bundles of joy are welcomed with love, it becomes concerning when parents, many still learning to care for themselves, say they feel unprepared or unwilling to take full responsibility for raising their children. The ripple effects of this unpreparedness are profound, impacting both the children and society.

While I understand that not every child can grow up with both biological parents, I firmly believe every child deserves a nurturing father or mother figure in their life. The absence of a father leaves an undeniable mark on a child's emotional, psychological, and social development. Although every individual's experience is unique, certain themes emerge repeatedly.

Emotional Scars and Their Long-Term Impact

Abandonment Issues:

The absence of a father often fosters feelings of abandonment, making it difficult for individuals to trust others in relationships. I have experienced this firsthand. I know someone who struggled to trust her partner, constantly chasing after him out of insecurity. In retrospect, she had both of her parents absent, and he shared a similar history. Their relationship, built on fragile ground, eventually fell apart. It became clear that both were grappling with unresolved wounds from their childhoods. As a parent, you do not want this for your child.

Low Self-Esteem:

Many children struggle with self-worth without the positive influence of a father's validation. For me, excelling in academics became my sole identity. While others admired themselves in mirrors, I found solace in music and my books, avoiding relating with people or even having beauty conversations because I felt ugly and unworthy for the longest time.

Depression and Anxiety:

Emotional voids can manifest as chronic depression or anxiety. I have met young people who have shared how the absence of a parent has left them battling these silent struggles. Research shows that children in single-parent households are nearly twice as likely to experience depressive symptoms compared to those in two-parent families.

(Psychology Today, NeuroLaunch.com)

Relationship Challenges

Difficulty Trusting Others:

Trust becomes a hurdle when a reliable father figure is absent. This has been an ongoing struggle for me, influencing romantic and platonic relationships.

Attachment Issues

Without a secure foundation, it can be hard to discern healthy connections. I have found myself attaching to the wrong people and constantly seeking validation I never received as a child.

Seeking Validation

Intentional parenting involves consistent validation, which builds confidence. Without it, children often seek approval from external sources. Despite my achievements, I have often longed for validation that should have come from within my family.

Identity Formation

Uncertain Identity

A father's guidance is integral to helping children understand their identity and place in the world. Without it, I felt lost. As a child, I disliked how I looked; I wished I was somebody else, struggled to belong, and wished I were part of a different family. Salvation and the church eventually helped me find my worth, but the journey was arduous.

Gender Role Confusion

The absence of a father figure often contributes to confusion about traditional gender roles. While society's views on roles evolve, I believe that some responsibilities inherently align with each gender. I have been deeply frustrated by encounters with men who lacked basic leadership skills or understanding of their roles, and I have seen women struggle with tasks they were never taught. Parenting should go beyond providing food and education; it must include deliberate training to prepare children for adulthood. Fathers play a vital role in modeling responsibility and teaching life skills through words and actions.

Educational and Career Challenges

Lack of Motivation:

A father's encouragement can inspire children to pursue ambitious goals. Without it, children may lack the drive to excel academically or professionally.

Financial Instability

Single-parent households often face financial strain, limiting access to resources and opportunities for education and growth.

Behavioral Issues

Risk-Taking Behavior:

Without proper guidance, some individuals may turn to risky behaviors to cope with emotional voids or unresolved feelings. For example, a teenager who lacks a supportive parental figure might experiment with substance use, believing it offers a temporary escape from their pain or loneliness.

Rebellion:

Without authority figures to provide structure, rebellion often becomes a way to express unresolved pain. I see many kids today who do things beyond their age out of rebellion. Though absurd, it is becoming prevalent in a culture that celebrates everything and continually degrades morality.

Negative Coping Mechanisms That Shape Our Lives

The absence of a father can have profound emotional and psychological effects, often leading children to adopt coping mechanisms that can shape their lives in unintended ways. While these behaviors may provide temporary relief, they often lead to further challenges in adulthood. Recognizing these patterns can help parents, educators, and mentors intervene early to foster healthier coping strategies.

1. Substance Abuse

For some, the emotional pain of rejection and abandonment becomes too much to bear, leading to substance abuse to numb the hurt. Statistics in the U.S. highlight that many teens without fathers turn to drugs in their late teens, seeking an escape from their unresolved pain. Addressing these root causes early can prevent children from falling into harmful patterns.

2. Eating Disorders

Emotional struggles tied to fatherlessness can also manifest as eating disorders. A child might attempt to gain control over their life through unhealthy eating habits, using food to cope with feelings of inadequacy and loss. Parents and guardians can help children develop healthier relationships with food and their emotions by creating a supportive environment and encouraging open conversations.

3. Promiscuity or Unhealthy Relationships:

Girls from father-absent homes are at higher risk of entering unhealthy or toxic relationships, often seeking validation and affection they lack from their fathers. A study published in Developmental Psychology found that early father absence is linked to an increased likelihood of earlier sexual activity and risky relationship behaviors. This connection is partly attributed to insecure attachment styles and lower self-esteem, which drive individuals to seek emotional fulfillment in unstable ways. The lack of a healthy male role model disrupts their understanding of balanced relationships, perpetuating cycles of emotional dependence and unhealthy partnerships.

4. Humor as a Defense Mechanism

Some children adopt humor to mask their inner pain, becoming class clowns or constantly joking to avoid vulnerability. While this may seem harmless, it prevents them from addressing deeper emotional wounds and forming authentic connections.

5. Hyper-Independence

Hyper-independence can emerge as a defense mechanism, with children determined to rely solely on themselves. While self-reliance is often celebrated, it can limit one's ability to trust or connect with others, creating barriers to meaningful relationships. As someone who has struggled with this, I understand the toll it takes; relationships thrive on reciprocity, and hyper-independence often sends the message that you do not need others, even when you do.

6. Emotional Numbing

To avoid the pain of their father's absence, some children suppress their emotions, becoming emotionally numb. They may act as if they do not care about personal relationships, but this detachment can lead to a lack of empathy and meaningful connections. Emotional numbness is dangerous, creating walls that are hard to break down.

7. Withdrawal or Isolation

The fear of abandonment can cause some children to withdraw from others, becoming emotionally closed off or socially isolated. While this may appear as shyness or introversion, it often masks deeper fears of rejection and disappointment. I can relate to this, as part of my reserved nature as a child stemmed from coping with early disappointments.

8. Anger and Aggression

For many, unresolved feelings of abandonment turn into anger, leading to outbursts toward peers, teachers, or family members. This aggression is often a cry for help, reflecting the frustration of feeling unsupported and unloved.

9. People-Pleasing

Some children become overly agreeable to avoid conflict and maintain affection. They aim to ensure that no one abandons them again, often at the expense of their own needs and boundaries. While this behavior may seem harmless, it can lead to burnout and resentment in adulthood.

10. Overachievement

Some children channel their emotional pain into becoming overachievers. They push themselves to excel in academics, sports, or extracurricular activities, hoping their success will fill the emotional void. While this drive can lead to impressive accomplishments, it often masks feelings of inadequacy and unworthiness.

Breaking the Cycle Through Awareness and Support

While these coping mechanisms are understandable, they do not have to define a child's future. With intentional efforts from parents, guardians, and mentors, we can help children develop healthier ways to process their emotions and build resilience.

It is important to note that not everyone who grows up with an absent parent will experience these challenges. Individuals can overcome adversity through resilience, support systems, and personal growth. Therapy, counseling, and positive mentorship can also play crucial roles in mitigating the effects of an absent father or mother and promoting healthy emotional development.

Positive Coping and Empowering the Fatherless

While the absence of a father can create emotional and social challenges, children can develop resilience and thrive when provided with the right support systems and opportunities. Below are strategies and coping mechanisms that empower fatherless children to build fulfilling and independent lives.

Strong Support Networks

Family and Extended Family: Building close relationships with relatives can provide children with emotional stability and a sense of belonging. These connections help reinforce the idea that they are loved and supported.

Community Support: Engaging with community organizations, mentors, or local churches can offer additional resources and social connections. These networks can foster a sense of community and reduce feelings of isolation.

Example: A local church youth group or sports team can be a valuable platform for forming supportive friendships and receiving guidance.

Counseling and Therapy

Professional Support: Mental health professionals can help children process feelings of loss and develop effective coping strategies tailored to their unique experiences.

Group Therapy: Joining peer-trusted support groups can create a safe space for children to share their struggles and gain insight from others who have faced similar challenges.

Example: A group therapy session might include activities focused on building trust and emotional expression, helping children feel understood and valued.

Engagement in Extracurricular Activities

Sports and Arts: Participating in sports, music, or art activities provides children with an outlet for self-expression and a chance to build teamwork and friendships.

Clubs and Organizations: Joining clubs like scouting, drama, or robotics can boost confidence, social skills, and achievement.

Example: A child who joins a soccer team learns discipline and teamwork and develops lasting friendships that foster emotional growth.

Education and Skill Development

Focus on Education: Encouraging academic success helps instill purpose and direction. Education serves as a foundation for personal growth and future opportunities.

Life Skills Training: Programs that teach essential skills, such as financial literacy, career planning, and time management, can empower children to build independent and fulfilling lives.

Example: A workshop on budgeting or job interview skills can equip children with the tools they need to navigate adulthood confidently.

Positive Role Models
Mentorship Programs
Connecting children with mentors who embody positive values and provide guidance can help fill the void of a father figure.

Community Leaders: Coaches, teachers, or local leaders can inspire children by offering encouragement, motivation, and real-life examples of success.

Example: A teacher who takes an active interest in a child's development can act as a role model and a source of stability.

Emotional Expression

Journaling: Encouraging children to keep a journal gives them a private outlet to process their thoughts and feelings. Writing can help them make sense of their emotions and build self-awareness.

Creative Outlets: Activities like painting, creative writing, or playing a musical instrument can be therapeutic tools, allowing children to channel their emotions into productive expressions.

Example: A child who enjoys writing stories may discover a passion that helps them process feelings while building self-confidence. I remember writing a lot as a child and throughout my teenage years.

Resilience Training

Building Coping Skills: Programs focused on resilience can teach children how to handle adversity, solve problems, and develop a growth mindset.

Fostering Optimism: Teaching children to reframe challenges as opportunities can empower them to face life confidently and positively.

Example: A resilience workshop might include role-playing scenarios to teach effective problem-solving and emotional regulation.

Fostering Independence and Responsibility

Age-Appropriate Responsibilities: Allowing children to take on tasks at home or in their community helps build self-esteem and a sense of accomplishment.

Encouraging Decision-Making: Involving children in decisions about their lives, such as choosing extracurricular activities or setting personal goals, fosters empowerment and self-worth.

Example: Assigning a child the responsibility of planning a family meal encourages independence while building valuable life skills.

Facing reality forced me to reevaluate what I believed about fatherhood and family. I realized that the brokenness I had experienced was not God's design. In His Word, I found a blueprint for fatherhood, a divine idea that calls men to lead, nurture, and protect. This revelation became a turning point in understanding my healing and God's purpose for families.

> "God calls men to be servant leaders in their homes,
> to sacrifice themselves for their wives and children,
> and to lead them with love and care."
> – John Piper

CHAPTER SIX

GOD'S IDEA

"Being a father means teaching your children the beauty of God's grace both through words and by example."
– Tim Keller.

One day, I argued with a family member about their parenting choices. I advocated for her children to spend some time with their father. Her response was sharp: "What is he adding to the children? Are they lacking anything?" Another time, she said, as some of you might also wonder, "Vivienne, what do you know about raising children?"

Let me address that question directly: I may not have all the experience you think I need, but I can share with you what has been revealed to me, what I have personally experienced and learned, and what is written in the Bible. This is not about proving expertise but helping where I can. You do not have to agree with me. I intend to save some from the unnecessary pain and struggles I have seen and experienced. At that moment, though, I was so hurt and frustrated that I vowed never to speak about her children again, God reminded me of my calling to care not just for one family but for generations. I had been "mothering" long before my natural desire for children existed.

This led me to reflect on the story of Jesus' birth. If fathers weren't important, as some of my relatives and others seem to believe, then why was Joseph chosen to be Jesus' earthly father? The Bible describes Joseph as a good man, and even when he considered breaking his engagement to Mary after he had learned that she was pregnant, God intervened through a dream and told him not to. Do we ever wonder if God just wanted to honor their engagement or if Jesus needed a father to be present? I believe Joseph had a significant role to play. There was an image to uphold, a legacy to carry, and a need for Joseph to fulfill his duties as a father, leading, providing, protecting, and nurturing. Though Jesus had a heavenly Father, God still ordained Joseph to model fatherhood on earth.

God's design for Jesus' life was intentional, down to the lineage from which He was born. Joseph's presence was not a coincidence but part of God's divine plan. And just as Jesus did not choose His earthly father, neither do we. God ordains these roles, and as believers, we must anchor our understanding of family and fatherhood on the foundation of the Word.

Marriage

In the book of Genesis, God gives them a purpose that extends beyond their existence after he created man and woman. Part of this purpose was to fill the earth and steward His creation. The Bible tells us in **Genesis 2:18 NIV, "It is not good for the man to be alone; I will make a helper suitable for him...."** God made Eve for Adam with intentionality and purpose. We see God being intentional about suitability; together, they were charged with being fruitful, multiplying, subduing the earth, and exercising dominion over all living things.

Before children entered the picture, man and woman were united before God. God brought them together, not the children. Children were the blessing that came after the man clung to his wife, when the two became one flesh. Eve was formed from Adam's rib to signify their inseparable bond, unity in purpose, and complementary roles.

This divine order is being challenged today. Many of us, whether through ignorance or conformity to the world's patterns of cohabitation, fornication, and other cultural deviations, have strayed from God's original design. But this was never God's intent. Marriage was His idea, a sacred covenant established to provide a secure and nurturing foundation for raising families. It is not merely a human institution but a divine arrangement intended for our benefit and flourishing. Following His design leads to blessings, stability, and alignment with His greater purpose for us.

God, as the ultimate Father, modeled provision, purpose, and order. He created man, revealed his purpose to him, gave him meaningful work, and then made him a partner in Eve. Together, their union had a calling beyond personal fulfilment; they were to steward God's creation and reproduce per His command. This was not about Adam being captivated solely by Eve's beauty or Eve seeking provision from Adam. Their relationship was not rooted in selfish desires like we see today in many of our relationships but in their shared purpose under God's design.

As God intended, marriage is not just for pleasure but for purpose. It is a partnership built on His love, agreement, stewardship, service, and calling. By aligning our lives with His plan, we find deeper meaning in our relationships and fulfill the roles He has designed for us.

You're His Own

The Bible does not describe the same enthusiasm and intentionality when God created the other creatures as when He created man. With humanity, in *Genesis 1:26 KJV*, God said, and *"Let us make man in our image, after our likeness."* This declaration reveals that God had a purpose for man as He crafted him in his own image. Man was special from the beginning; he was not an afterthought but God's idea and masterpiece.

Before you became a parent, you were and still are a child of God, whom He intentionally created and delights in. You are not here by accident or coincidence. Even when humanity disrupted God's order through sin, He demonstrated His love by sending His Son, Jesus, to restore what was broken. Jesus purchased humanity with His blood, making salvation and reconciliation with God possible for all who believe. This is how precious you are to God. He values you so deeply that He gave everything to bring you back to Himself.

You matter profoundly to God. He not only created you with care but has also provided for you in immeasurable ways, starting with the forgiveness of your sins, past, present, and future, through faith in Jesus. God's love is unconditional and sacrificial. He gave His only Son, not as a spare or afterthought but as His most precious gift for your redemption.

Before living as a godly parent, you must first embrace God's heart toward you. He sees you, loves you, and has never stopped caring for you. Many people wrestle with feelings of inadequacy as parents, believing they have failed or fallen short. These thoughts can lead to guilt, self-hatred, depression, and even destructive behaviors. But those lies are not from God; they are from the enemy.

God's love for you is steadfast and unchanging. He has good plans for you and your family. You are not defined by your mistakes or shortcomings but by God's eternal love and purpose for your life. Forgive yourself, believe in His promises, and receive the unconditional love He freely gives. As you embrace His love, you will find the strength, grace, and wisdom to lead your family well.

Never forget that you matter to God. He created you with intention, loves you without condition, and has equipped you for the journey ahead. You are not your own; you were bought at a price.

Children Are A Blessing

The Bible is clear: children are a blessing from God. Whether things happen according to God's ordained order for family or not, children are never a mistake. I have had conversations where people have told me, "This child was a mistake; I did not plan to have him/her! "Whether you planned it or not, God expects us to receive and treat them as the blessings they are. The Bible says *in Psalm 127:3 (CEV): "Children are a blessing and a gift from the Lord."*

I understand many of us were not planned but look at what God has made of us! Look at His faithfulness over your life! I remember one day complaining about how hard I was working, and my mum used a trending notion in Uganda at the time. She told me, "You have to work because you're not a planned kid; you're not like those kids who were planned and have inheritances from their parents." Hahaha. Believing or feeling alone and unplanned, like my mom says, is tempting, but we ultimately belong to God. It does not matter how, why, or where you were conceived; God knows you and has a purpose for you! Jeremiah 1:5 (NIV) says, *"Before I formed you in the womb, I knew you before you were born, I set you apart; I appointed you as a prophet to the nations."*

In the same way, I deeply sympathize and understand that some parenthood comes through painful circumstances like rape or defilement. That is not God's idea. While God can work through pain, He does not inflict it on us. Knowing that God did not cause you those predicaments is important for those in such situations. I pray for thorough healing and comfort, and I encourage you to look to God for healing because it is His will to heal you. Also, seek godly counsel or medical help where necessary. Find a safe community, like a church, where you can overcome such trauma and thrive in your parenthood.

Isaiah 61 speaks about how God gives beauty for ashes, joy for mourning, and praise for the spirit of heaviness so that we might be called trees of righteousness, planted by the Lord, that He might be glorified. This promise is for you, too! I commend you to God and His truth; only through it can you unlearn, heal, and rebuild. Believe that your child is a blessing.

Do not curse them, and do not curse yourself; there is hope for you and your child. The Bible says Jesus Christ is a living hope to those who believe. Declare, "My Redeemer lives; I will rise again," one day, you will testify after triumphantly training your child in the way of the Lord.

Proverbs 22:6 (KJV) says, "Train up a child in the way he should go, and when he is old, he will not depart from it."

> *"Some fathers are absent from their children's lives due to the drama stirred up by their wives or the mother of their children. I wish women would provide these men with a smoother path to be present for their kids, not for the sake of the adults but for the children's sake. Every child needs a father figure in their life. If you deny a father access to his child, it is something you'll regret because those missed moments are irreplaceable. Once they're gone, they do not come back, no matter what stage in life you're in."*
>
> *- Eddie. K. S at Photizo Daily.*

God Is a God of Order

God is a God of order, and much of the brokenness we see in our generation stems from our deviation from His design. As the Master Creator, He upholds the universe; whether we acknowledge Him or not, we are His creation. This means that creating and raising children was always meant to align with His purposes. Yet today, even within the church, some of us have disregarded His principles concerning family and relationships. As a result, the challenges of raising children following God's way have grown more evident.

First, as the church, can we return to the foundations and the truth of the Word of God? Can we be more deliberate and teach about family, marriage, and relationships, considering the rampant fatherlessness today, to equip young people before we push them into commitments they don't understand? Can we have more conversations about God's order for family, the readiness required, and the responsibility involved in marriage? I have honestly been frustrated over the years by many older people who keep pressuring us for weddings and children, and some go ahead and judge us without ever sitting down to ask and know the story of our lives. Do we want to count weddings, or do we surely care about our well-being, marriage, and family?

God's design for the family has always been clear: a man and a woman joined in marriage, forming the foundation for raising children. While this may be unpopular in today's culture, it is important to recognize that the destruction of marriage and family is a deliberate strategy by the enemy to weaken generations and undermine the church. As believers, we must consciously evaluate whether our inherited or adopted patterns align with God's truth or reflect societal norms.

For three years, I hesitated to publish this book. During that time, I extensively explored the patterns within my own family. While I do not claim to have it all figured out, I am confident I am already breaking certain generational cycles by the grace of God, who revealed this book to me. The reality is that just because something is widely accepted does not make it right. As children of God, we are called to live by His manual for life, His Word. Before dismissing the importance of marriage in raising children, ask yourself: What does the Bible say? What does God say? Are you following Jesus, or merely following trends?

From my experience, while sin is forgiven, its consequences often linger. Many of us suffer not from ignorance but from knowingly choosing paths that deviate from God's will. My pastor, Tom Kiessling, once said**, "Sin is complicated and makes life a mess. When we transgress God's ways, we invite drama and unnecessary struggles into our lives."** The weight of those choices can be heavy. Whether judged by others or not, we inevitably reap what we sow.

While there are exceptions to every situation, God's design remains unchanging and eternally true. This isn't about judgment but reflection. If something is out of order in our lives or generation, we must bring it back in line with God's Word. Some may argue, "Not all children of married couples grow up well." That may be true, but it does not negate God's original design. Family is the foundational structure of society, and His intent was for fathers and mothers to work together in agreement to raise children.

You might ask, "What about breakups, separation, divorce, and toxic relationships?" While God hates divorce, He does not endorse abuse in any form. His desire is for us to live in peace with one another. The Bible commands us to pursue peace with all men; remarkably, God even calls us to forgive those who have hurt us and love our enemies. These aren't suggestions; they are commands from our loving Father.

Does this mean you should stay in an abusive relationship? Not. Decisions about whether to leave or stay must be made prayerfully and in alignment with God's guidance. God is our ultimate authority and protector and desires peace and safety for children. Whatever decision you make, remember His ideal way of raising children: in love, unity, and admonition of His Word.

My heart goes out to those who have endured the pain of breakups or divorce. Please know that God sees you, understands your struggles, and can be trusted to guide you through your journey. Remember that your children are blessings and deserve the love and care of their mother and father. Even amidst life's challenges, God's design for family remains a beacon of hope and restoration.

Work It Out

Parents are stewards entrusted by God to care for children. While it is essential to prioritize your well-being, we must never lose sight of the fact that children are gifts from God. Parenting is a partnership with Him, a divine responsibility to nurture, guide, and train children as the bible commands. I empathize heartily with those who had little to no choice in how things unfolded. Still, I have also observed many of us sometimes making selfish decisions without fully considering the impact on these precious lives, especially during separations from the other parent.

I remember a conversation with my mother about the time she separated from my dad. She reflected on how, amid their struggles, both did not pause to ask how their separation would affect us, the children. She admitted, **"When you're a young mother, there is so much you do not know."** These reflections stayed with me, highlighting the gaps in how decisions are often made. God's design was for parents to actively and intentionally partner in raising their children financially, physically, emotionally, and spiritually.

Children need both parents. It is not just about the basics like food and shelter but about presence, connection, and shared responsibility. It deeply saddens me to see situations where one parent, often the mother, cuts off the father entirely sometimes because they feel financially independent enough to manage without him. But fatherhood is not solely about financial provision. Fathers offer so much more than what money can buy. Their presence fulfills an irreplaceable emotional and developmental need. This truth is at the heart of God's design for the family.

Children need their fathers as providers, protectors, role models, and nurturers. Substituting a father's role with material provision, thinking it will fill the gap, does not work. The void left by a missing father figure is real and has long-lasting effects. That said, I also firmly believe that God, in His goodness, can provide consistent father figures or lead someone to adopt and love a child as his own.

Still, whether out of ignorance or selfishness, denying children access to the other parent is harmful. This book is my heartfelt plea to parents, especially mothers: children need their fathers, no matter what. You might say, "Vivienne, you do not know what I have been through or how abusive that man was." And you're right, and I do not know your story. But God does. He calls us to forgive and to live in peace, not only for our healing but for the well-being of our children.

I am not suggesting that anyone should remain in a toxic or abusive partnership. Safety and peace must come first. But I urge you to seek an amicable path to co-parenting. Speak with trusted elders or counselors who can guide you through the complexities of your situation. Remember, as parents, we are stewards; these children ultimately belong to God. He can grant you the grace and wisdom to navigate even the most challenging circumstances. He is faithful.

I write this not from a place of judgment but from the perspective of someone who has lived through the pain and emptiness of knowing her father was alive yet absent. I write as someone still healing and wants future generations to avoid the deep wounds that fatherlessness leaves behind. Let us do our part to ensure that children grow up whole, surrounded by love, and guided by God's truth.

Proverbs 3:5-6 NLT reminds us, *"Trust in the Lord with all your heart; do not depend on your own understanding. Seek his will in all you do, and he will show you which path to take."* Trust God through the process. Let Him teach you how to co-parent. Ask Him for the grace to cooperate for the sake of this generation He has entrusted to us.

I recognize that some of us have been in abusive or toxic relationships where it is only safe for the children to be apart from their toxic parents. In such situations, do not try to bear the burden alone. Ask God to carry you through it and believe in a new life. God is our ever-present help in times of trouble. Just as He speaks in Isaiah 43:2 (NLT*), "When you go through deep waters, I will be with you. When you go through rivers of difficulty, you will not drown. When you walk through the fire of oppression, you will not be burned up; the flames will not consume you."*

Believe that God will bring father figures into your children's lives. Do not try to be everything to them. Allow God to guide and direct you on how to raise them intentionally. Seek community in the church, extended family, or other support networks. Allow yourself to heal, love, and be loved, or even remarry if you choose. God's design for family is agape love, a hedge of protection over you and your children.

In the Way They Should Go

I have seen and heard countless stories about parents who, out of unresolved pain and anger toward their ex-partners, unintentionally transfer those emotions onto their children. This behavior leaves lasting damage, whether through harsh words, dismissive actions, or directly teaching their children to resent the other parent. A wise friend once told me, "If you do not have anything good to say about someone, do not say anything at all." This advice is particularly vital when it comes to co-parenting. Speaking ill of the other parent harms not just their image in your child's eyes; it poisons your child's heart.

Instead, strive to guard your child's innocence. Allow their conscience toward their other parents to remain untainted. Speak with love, patience, and understanding, and let your children form their own opinions based on their experiences. They do not need to bear the weight of your unresolved emotions. As hard as it might be, let love be your language, ensuring your words and actions nurture their hearts, not burden them with bitterness.

Parenting is a sacred stewardship. From conception, seeking God's guidance for your child's life is crucial. Ask Him for clarity about His plans and begin praying over them even while they are still in the womb. Studies show that babies can hear and respond to external stimuli before birth, so let the words they hear be words of blessing, affirmation, and love. Fathers, your role starts early. Let your child hear your voice, feel your presence, and know your commitment. Engage actively in their journey, even before they take their first breath.

In today's world, where societal values often blur the lines of right and wrong, children are given unchecked freedom that can lead to harm. As parents, we are responsible for following God's blueprint for raising them. Establish clear family values and boundaries and communicate your non-negotiables with love and consistency. These values are not about control but providing children with a secure foundation for navigating life's challenges.

Fathers, your role is irreplaceable. Providing financially is important, but your presence and active involvement in every season of your child's life are even more vital. Lead your family in prayer, Bible study, and meaningful conversations. Be present not just physically but emotionally and spiritually. Model godly behavior so your children can see what walking in faith and integrity is. Remember, children learn more from what they see you do than you tell them.

In a world filled with distractions and broken relationships, your commitment as a parent to nurture, guide, and pray for your children can be the difference between a life filled with purpose and one led astray. It is not what you leave for them; it is what you leave in them. Let us rise to the call of parenthood as God intended, becoming the stewards our children need and deserve.

New/Blended Families

I have witnessed many men reject their children simply because their relationships with the children's mothers ended. Whether out of anger, resentment, or the desire to move on and create new families, these men often choose to forget or pretend to forget their first children. I struggle to understand how a "God-fearing man" can wake up each day, go about his life, and yet feel no sense of responsibility or longing for his child. In their attempts to hurt or spite their ex-partners, they fail to see the profound and lasting pain they are inflicting on their children. Children need their fathers financially, emotionally, spiritually, and physically. A child needs to hear their father's affirmations, feel his presence, and know his love.

Sending money isn't enough. Relying on the fact that the child's mother is wealthy is not an excuse to be absent. Fathers must actively participate in their children's lives; children deserve nothing less. God chose you to be their father for a reason. Stop playing games with this sacred responsibility. You do not need material wealth to be a good dad; your presence matters most. Your children will not remember the mansions or cars but the moments you shared and the lessons you taught. Purpose in your heart to become the father God intended you to be.

It also pains me deeply to see women marry men who are single dads but then alienate or reject their stepchildren. Blending families can undoubtedly be complex, but it is not impossible; many incredible women have done it successfully. If you're unwilling or unprepared to embrace your husband's children, why marry him? How can you be happy in a marriage where your husband neglects his other children, and you do nothing to help him fulfill his role as their father? A godly woman is a helper to her husband, not just for his benefit but for the benefit of his children. Some women do not only stop at not being unsupportive but continue to abuse these children. Even if you can't replace their mother or do not have a good relationship with her, the children are innocent and still deserve love, guidance, and stability.

As a mother, how can you live comfortably in a home supported by your husband's income, knowing he hasn't sent a penny to his other children? As a God-fearing wife who knows children are a blessing, you shouldn't get in his way but remind him of his responsibilities. I believe it honors God and contributes to raising a generation of whole, unbroken individuals. I pray for a generation of secure, confident women unafraid of their husbands maintaining healthy co-parenting relationships with their ex-partners.

Likewise, men who marry women with children must be prepared to love and accept those children as their own. Do not pursue the relationship if you're not ready to adopt or positively influence her children's lives. I have heard too many heartbreaking stories of men who mistreat their wife's older children, making them "pay in kind" for the sacrifices they feel they've made. Such behavior is cruel. Even if the biological parent does not see the abuse, God does.

Blended families should be built on the foundation of God's love and fear. Let God guide your actions and decisions. Children should never have to hate themselves or suffer because of the choices their parents made. If you build a blended family, commit to being a source of love, stability, and healing for all the children involved. They deserve nothing less.

Just Be a Parent: Stop Trying to Be a Super-mom or Super-dad

Many parents, out of pride or hurt, cut off their children's other parent to prove that they can do it all on their own. While this might appear noble or strong, parenting is not about winning a competition. It is not about proving who can do more or is more important. Once, I spoke with a single mom who was stuck and financially struggling. I suggested she contact her children's father for help, but she firmly refused. She said she would rather remain stuck than let him know she was struggling. I couldn't believe it; why let pride or unresolved issues stand in the way of getting support for the children? God designed parenting as a shared responsibility, with each parent playing a unique and irreplaceable role.

You cannot outdo the role God intended for both parents to fulfill, no matter how capable you are. Parenting is not about control; it is about stewardship. Your children are not your property; they are gifts entrusted to you by God. Commit them to His guidance and allow Him to work through others, including your co-parents, friends, and family.

Refusing to involve the other parent does not erase their existence. Unless someone else legally adopts your children, they will always be connected to the parent you denied them. While children may feel hurt or anger toward an absent parent as they grow, reconciliation is often inevitable. And when that happens, all your efforts to keep them apart may be meaningless. Ironically, the absent parents, those who contributed nothing to their children's upbringing, often feel entitled to their children's success later in life.

Let me share my experience. Though my mother carried almost all the responsibility of raising us, it did not stop my father from seeking help when I became financially independent. And I obliged. When my father passed away, I grieved deeply, as though I had grown up with him by my side. Despite our limited relationship, the pain was excruciating; I felt compelled to do everything I could for him, even in death. In a short period, I spent more on him than I ever had on myself or anyone else. But it was too late, no matter how much I wanted to do. He was gone. I often hear women say their children's fathers should never rely on their kids for anything in the future. However, I beg to differ from experience. The parent who isn't contributing now or whom you've cut off may one day become more demanding than you. My experience taught me a powerful lesson: parenting is not a competition. You do not need to prove anything to anyone. Just by being a loving and present parent, you've already succeeded. Parenting is not something to be done in isolation. Seek help. Surround yourself with relatives, community members, and support groups who can offer guidance and companionship.

Raising a child alone is overwhelming, and you shouldn't have to carry that burden by yourself. This is also a call to those in our communities: if you know a single parent, even one who seems to have everything under control, step in and offer help. Love their children, answer their questions, and bless them with whatever kindness God has equipped you to give. Parenting is a shared journey, not just between the parents but also within a community. Together, we can raise children to be whole, loved, and prepared for life.

This book may not answer all the parental issues we face in our generation. However, if you and I can purposefully follow God's idea of parenting, we can save one and then another until we save an entire generation. I need you to know that you matter regardless of where you find yourself as a parent or someone who hopes to be a parent. Do not forget that your children's well-being depends on you, so take care of yourself, but do not be selfish. Choose your children, choose God, and choose His plan. God is a God of contingencies. He never runs out of solutions, so trust Him. Remember, raising your children God's way is not a want but a need. Make it work. Amen.

Understanding God's divine design for fatherhood was an eye-opening revelation. It gave me a renewed perspective on the role of fathers, not just as providers or disciplinarians but as leaders, protectors, and nurturers, reflecting God's heart for His children. Yet, the reality of fatherhood in our world often falls short of this ideal. Many fathers are absent emotionally or physically, leaving voids that shape their children's lives in profound ways. This brings us to the question: what does true fatherhood look like, and why does it matter so much?

> *"A father's love paints a picture for his children of what God's love is like preparing them to know their Heavenly Father."*
> *– Louie Giglio*

CHAPTER SEVEN

FATHERHOOD

> *"Fathers, your children are not just watching your behavior; they are watching to see what you believe about God based on how you live."*
> – Voddie Baucham.

Fatherhood is far more than the biological act of parenthood. It is a profound commitment to guiding, nurturing, and supporting a child's development in every aspect of life. A father's role extends beyond providing care and protection; it is about being a constant source of love, wisdom, and discipline. Fatherhood requires presence, leadership, and the responsibility of shaping a child's moral, social, and spiritual growth.

A true father is a positive role model, offering stability and direction while empowering children to navigate the complexities of life. Across cultures and faiths, fatherhood is revered as a vital foundation for a child's journey to becoming a mature, responsible adult. It is a partnership between love and accountability, instilling values that will echo throughout a child's life and beyond.

Absent Dads

Absent fathers, or absentee dads, are physically or emotionally unavailable in their children's lives. This absence can stem from a range of circumstances: separation, divorce, abandonment, incarceration, work commitments, or even death. At times, an absent father may live under the same roof as his children yet fail to engage emotionally, leaving a void where nurturing and support should be.

Fathers, when you neglect or are forced by circumstances to stay away from your children, you leave them vulnerable to malicious people. They face this hostile world without your guidance, letting whoever cares to decide how to treat them. Without your protection, your daughter risks entering relationships where she is undervalued or even mistreated. The absence of a father's love and presence robs her of the blueprint for how a man should treat her, with respect, care, and dignity. I have been through all this and don't want it for your child.

The Emotionally Absent Father: A Silent Wound

An emotionally absent father is physically present but disengaged from his child's life. He may prioritize work, hobbies, or personal interests over building a meaningful connection with his child. His emotional unavailability creates a silent wound, often leaving the child feeling neglected, unheard, and undervalued.

Signs of Emotional Absence

- Lack of Communication: He rarely inquiries about his daughter's day, feelings, or aspirations. Conversations, if they occur, are superficial and marked by short, distracted responses, leaving the child feeling unseen and unheard.
- Absence of Affection: An emotionally absent father avoids physical and verbal expressions of love, such as hugs or words of affirmation. This lack of affection can foster loneliness and low self-esteem in the child.

- Avoidance of Conflict and Difficult Conversations: Instead of guiding his child through challenges, he withdraws or dismisses her concerns. This avoidance teaches her that her problems are insignificant and that she must navigate them alone.
- Prioritization of Other Activities: Such fathers may devote most of their time to work, hobbies, or personal pursuits, leaving little room for meaningful interaction with their children.
- Missing Key Events: An emotionally absent father often misses milestones such as school plays, sports games, or parent-teacher meetings. Frequent no-shows, whether due to broken promises or unspoken priorities, send a message of neglect.

Moving Forward: Bridging the Emotional Gap

Parents who recognize their emotional absence can begin fostering healthier, more fulfilling relationships with their children. It starts with acknowledging the gaps and making a concerted effort to show up physically and emotionally. For mothers and guardians, introducing positive father figures, such as mentors, uncles, or trusted family friends, can help fill the void for children who lack a present father.

The Abusive Father: A Source of Harm

An abusive father causes significant harm through physical, emotional, psychological, or verbal abuse. This toxic behavior leaves lasting scars on a child's development, often shaping their self-esteem, relationships, and worldview well into adulthood.

Characteristics of an Abusive Father

- **Control and Domination:** Abusive fathers often assert authority through fear, intimidation, or manipulation, demanding unquestioning obedience.

- **Physical Abuse:** This includes any form of physical harm, from hitting and beating to using excessive force. Even threats of violence can create an atmosphere of constant fear.

- **Emotional Manipulation:** Using guilt, shame, or belittling language, abusive fathers erode a child's self-esteem, making them feel inadequate or incapable.

- **Verbal Abuse:** Constant yelling, insults, name-calling, and criticism can leave children feeling degraded and unloved, with emotional scars as deep as those caused by physical abuse.

- **Neglect:** Abusive fathers may ignore their child's emotional, physical, or developmental needs, leaving the child feeling abandoned and unworthy.

- **Unpredictability and Mood Swings:** Sudden, explosive reactions create an unstable home environment, forcing children to live in fear of triggering the next outburst.

- **Lack of Empathy:** Abusive fathers often disregard their children's feelings, focusing solely on their needs and desires.

- **Blaming and Denial:** Instead of taking responsibility, abusive fathers often blame their children for their abusive actions, claiming the child "deserved" it.

- **Isolation:** Preventing the child from building relationships or seeking outside support deepens their dependence on the abusive parent and isolates them from help.

Children raised in abusive environments often face lifelong challenges, including low self-esteem, trust issues, and difficulty regulating emotions. The effects of abuse do not end in childhood; they ripple into adulthood, influencing relationships, career paths, and overall well-being.

Father Figures

"A good father is one of the most unsung, un-praised, unnoticed, and yet one of the most valuable assets in our society."

– Billy Graham.

A father figure is a man who plays a pivotal role in a child's life, offering guidance, support, and nurturing. This figure may not always be the biological father; he could be a mentor, role model, or caregiver who steps into the paternal role. Father figures provide stability, encouragement, and protection, influencing a child's values, beliefs, and behaviors through their consistent presence and thoughtful guidance.

I recognize the profound impact of father and mother figures on shaping future generations, and I urge those who feel called to step into mentorship roles. Boys need to be guided into becoming responsible men, while girls need nurturing to embrace their identities as women with confidence and purpose. Such mentorship is about teaching practical skills and instilling values that will anchor these children in life.

I have observed the success of similar initiatives in African American communities, where mentorship programs have uplifted countless young people. I hope that by the end of this book, more Ugandans and other communities, especially elders, will be inspired to take up this mantle. By making themselves available as mentors and role models, they can become beacons of hope and light to the fatherless, creating positive change that will last for generations.

Importance of a Father Figure for Daughters

A father figure plays an irreplaceable role in shaping a daughter's emotional, social, and psychological development. Here are some key areas where his influence is crucial:

Emotional Support:

A father figure provides a foundation of emotional stability, fostering a daughter's sense of security and self-worth. His presence encourages her to express and process emotions healthily, equipping her to navigate complex feelings confidently.

Role Modeling:

A father models the behavior daughters come to expect in their relationships by treating others with respect and kindness. His interactions set a standard for healthy, respectful partnerships, shaping her expectations for future connections.

Boosting Self-Esteem and Confidence:

Positive reinforcement from a father figure can profoundly impact a daughter's self-esteem. His encouragement and belief in her capabilities empower her to pursue her ambitions, tackle challenges, and embrace her strengths.

Identity Formation:

Fathers contribute significantly to their daughters' understanding of who they are. Through shared experiences, meaningful conversations, and guidance, daughters explore their interests, values, and beliefs, forming a strong sense of identity.

Developing Social Skills:

A father figure's presence allows daughters to learn essential social skills. Observing how he communicates and handles relationships offers valuable lessons in interpersonal dynamics that can be applied in friendships, work, and beyond.

Academic and Career Success:

Fathers actively supporting their daughters' education and career aspirations contribute to their academic achievements and professional growth. Encouragement, constructive feedback, and guidance help daughters build the confidence to pursue their goals.

Building Emotional Resilience:

Life is full of obstacles, and a father figure is pivotal in teaching daughters how to cope with challenges. His support during tough times fosters resilience, helping them develop inner strength and adaptability.

Teaching Healthy Boundaries:

A father figure provides a framework for understanding relationships' boundaries, respect, and assertiveness. He equips his daughter with the tools to maintain healthy interactions in various aspects of her life. The influence of a supportive and involved father figure extends far beyond childhood.

It lays the groundwork for a daughter's well-being, instills confidence, and prepares her for meaningful relationships and success in her personal and professional life. A father's guidance is about teaching life skills and shaping a future where his daughter thrives with the tools, values, and emotional resilience to lead a fulfilling life.

I am an Adopted Grandchild

In May 2023, I was overwhelmed by life's demands. I had just transitioned to a new career, juggled intensive classes, searched for an elusive apartment, and managed my personal life while working. My mind was racing, and I had little time for distractions or personal connections. Even my mother's endless enthusiasm to speak to me always felt like a chore to entertain during that season.

One morning, my mom asked me to help her raise funds for something she wanted to purchase. For once, I declined. My finances were stretched thin, and I could not spare anything as I searched for a new apartment. That same morning, I had scheduled a tour of a potential apartment with a leasing agent, holding onto the hope that it might be the breakthrough I desperately needed.

However, upon arriving at the location, the agent was nowhere to be found. If you know me, you understand how much I value time and how frustrated I felt then. With my patience running out and a mountain of responsibilities waiting, I turned on my Lyft driver app to squeeze in some extra earnings before work.

The Serendipitous Meeting

My first ride request was one I nearly canceled. I waited for what felt like forever, trying to contact the passenger without success. As I was leaving, I spotted an older man running toward my car. Against my better judgment, I waited, and he climbed in.

As I drove, I turned on my IT tutorials, mentally replaying my apartment tour debacle and strategizing my next steps. The man interrupted a few minutes into the ride, asking if I knew anything about phones. Initially hesitant to engage, I asked why he needed help. He explained that his old flip phone had died, possibly due to the volume of messages he had received.

Seven years with the same phone? I was impressed. I tried charging his phone with my multi-pin charger, but it did not work. He explained that the phone was his only way to communicate with his elderly services company for transportation and medical appointments.

Though I had no intention of getting involved, his predicament struck a chord. At that moment, I was thinking about my mum's request, which I had rejected, and the fact that I needed a new phone. Yet, as someone who values independence, I empathized with his dilemma of needing to rely on neighbors for something as basic as a phone call. When he mentioned the possibility of getting a new phone, I made a spontaneous decision and offered to get him one.

An Angel in Disguise

My offer astounded him, and he exclaimed, "Are you an angel?"

I smiled and replied, "No."

He then said, "God must have sent you; there is a place for you in heaven."

So, we changed routes and found a phone store, and after two hours of setup, he had a new phone identical to his old one. Though my day had been chaotic, I felt surprisingly calm. Perhaps this was what God wanted me to do all along, to be calm!

A Relationship Blossoms

That encounter marked the beginning of an extraordinary relationship. Two weeks later, I invited him to church. That Sunday was Mother's Day, and though his coming to church was just enough for me, he also gifted me a pink teddy bear, saying it was for my future children. hahaha.

I introduced him to my mum, and since then, Mr. Simmons has become part of my family, referring to me as his "muzzukulu" (grandchild).

Over the past year, we've shared countless moments of wisdom, laughter, and support. He has been a grandfather figure I did not have and did not know I needed, teaching me invaluable lessons about life, generosity, and resilience.

Three Lessons I Treasure

1. Faith and Trust in God

Despite almost being my grandma's age, Mr. Simmons has a zeal for God that inspires me. He often asks me questions about faith and Scripture, trusting my guidance. When his close friend was on life support, he asked me to pray and share God's word with him, and I went to the hospital, amazed by his determination to call me to pray!

I prayed, and he felt better, but later on, he passed because he didn't want to go through all the doctors' procedures on life support. Watching Mr. Simmons navigate the loss of his friend with remarkable grace reminded me of the strength we all need during trying times that only come from trusting God.

2. Conversations I Never Had

Mr. Simmons speaks to me in ways no man ever has, offering guidance without judgment. He often encourages me to get married, emphasizing honesty, love, and care as essential traits in a partner.

He said, "I do not want you to be alone like me; it is not good. I want you to have your own family." His words resonate deeply, filling a void left by my father's absence.

Another time, he brought me a new backpack and told me to save it for my future children, whom he hopes to babysit one day. He even, asked if he could walk me down the aisle as he explained to me how it is done in the American culture and proudly declared that he already had his suit ready, hahaha! While I laughed, I cherished the thought of him, though I have always dreamt of my mom walking me down the aisle.

3. Genuine Care and Concern

Mr. Simmons advises me on safety and self-care, showing a concern that touches my heart. Though I do not always follow everything he advises, I appreciate him for always looking out for me, and I know he genuinely cares. His generosity, kindness, and wisdom remind me of God's provision during challenging seasons of life.

A Divine Gift

Though Mr. Simmons calls me an angel sent by God, as he says I found him in a dark place, I believe he is my angel, a grandfather I did not know I needed. His life stories, generosity, and unwavering faith have profoundly impacted me. He taught me to slow down, trust God, and embrace life's unexpected blessings.

The week I met him, everything else fell into place. I found the apartment I was searching for, and my life gained a renewed sense of clarity and purpose. Mr. Simmons has been a living testament to God's ability to provide exactly what we need, even when we do not realize we need it.

I hope we can all read or listen to his life story one day. He is a testimony! May everyone have the privilege of encountering such a gift in their lives. Amen.

Fatherlessness in Uganda and the USA: Facts, Causes, and Impacts

Fatherlessness, the condition in which children grow up without a father figure, is a global issue with profound implications for society, family structures, and children's well-being. Whether caused by cultural norms, economic challenges, or social changes, the absence of a father figure impacts children's emotional health, academic performance, and future relationships. This section examines fatherlessness in Uganda and the United States, exploring its causes and analyzing its consequences over time.

Fatherlessness in Uganda is rooted in a combination of historical and ongoing challenges, including the HIV/AIDS epidemic, economic migration, cultural norms like polygamy, and the effects of conflict. While progress has been made in some areas, such as reducing HIV prevalence, many children still grow up without a father due to systemic and cultural factors.

HIV/AIDS Epidemic

1990s: Uganda was one of the countries hardest hit by the HIV/AIDS crisis, with an adult prevalence rate of approximately 15%. This epidemic resulted in widespread fatherlessness, with millions of children losing one or both parents. Uganda's aggressive public health campaigns and antiretroviral distribution helped reduce the prevalence rate significantly.

Now: By 2023, HIV prevalence had dropped to 5.4% (UNAIDS), but the epidemic's legacy persists. Around 1.2 million children in Uganda have lost one or both parents to AIDS, with many growing up fatherless.

Poverty and Economic Migration

1990s: Economic migration was prevalent due to political instability and economic stagnation caused by years of dictatorship and civil unrest. Many men migrated to urban areas for work, leaving families behind and contributing to fatherlessness.

Now: Despite economic improvements, poverty remains widespread, with 21% of the population living below the poverty line (World Bank, 2022). Economic migration continues to disrupt family structures as men leave to find work.

Cultural Norms and Polygamy

The 1990s: Polygamy, especially in rural areas, contributed to fatherlessness, as fathers with multiple households often had limited involvement in their children's lives.

Now, while modernization has slightly reduced polygamy in urban areas, the practice persists in rural regions, perpetuating fragmented family structures.

Political Instability and Conflict

1990s: The Lord's Resistance Army (LRA) conflict devastated northern Uganda, displacing families and resulting in countless fatherless children.

Now, although the LRA conflict has subsided, the impact lingers. Communities in northern Uganda continue to grapple with the legacy of fatherlessness caused by war-related deaths and displacements.

Alcohol Abuse and Selfishness

Alcohol abuse remains a significant factor in fatherlessness in Uganda. With one of the highest alcohol consumption rates in Africa (WHO, 2014), many fathers struggle with addiction, leading to neglect and absenteeism. Selfishness also plays a role, as some fathers prioritize personal interests over family responsibilities.

Societal Divisions

Differences in beliefs, political views, and social issues have separated families. Corruption, envy, and malice within communities force some individuals to flee for safety, further fragmenting families and leaving children without paternal guidance. Many immigrants here left their country due to such divisions, as countless people have lost their lives for holding different views on politics, religion, and cultural values.

Increased Toxic Relationships and Marriages

The prevalence of fatherlessness in Uganda has been significantly influenced by interpersonal dynamics, childhood trauma, and teen pregnancies. Marrying for the wrong reasons and a lack of commitment and responsibility in the family has led to a rise in broken families. As people try to escape such grounds of unhealthy relationships, some kids end up fatherless.

Fatherlessness in the United States

In the U.S., the increase in single-parent households, out-of-wedlock births, incarceration, and divorce reflects shifts in societal norms and structural challenges. While the divorce rate has declined slightly, fatherlessness continues to rise due to other compounding factors.

Divorce and Separation

Cause: Divorce and separation are the leading causes of fatherlessness. In many cases, after a divorce, fathers either lose custody or become less involved in their children's lives.

Statistic: 40-50% of marriages in the U.S. end in divorce, and 60% of children whose parents divorce live with their mother, resulting in the father's absence. (American Psychological Association, 2020)

Non-Residential Fathers

Cause: Even when fathers do not live with their children, they may not stay involved. Many non-custodial fathers do not maintain regular contact with their children.

Statistic: Only about 27% of non-residential fathers see their children regularly, and around half of non-custodial fathers are not involved in their children's lives. (U.S. Census Bureau, 2020)

Incarceration

Cause: Incarceration leads to fathers being physically absent from their children's lives, significantly contributing to fatherlessness.

Statistic: Over 2 million fathers in the U.S. are incarcerated, and 1 in 4 children have had a father incarcerated at some point in their life. (National Institute of Justice, 2023)

Teenage or Unplanned Pregnancies

Cause: Unplanned or teenage pregnancies often result in fathers being absent, either because they are too young or not prepared to assume parental responsibilities.

Statistic: 82% of teen fathers do not live with their children by age 5. (National Fatherhood Initiative, 2021)

Substance Abuse and Addiction

Cause: Fathers struggling with substance abuse may be unable to care for their children properly or may choose to leave, contributing to fatherlessness.

Statistic: 11% of fathers experience substance abuse disorders, which often leads to absenteeism or neglect. (National Institute on Drug Abuse, 2020)

Fatherlessness profoundly impacts children and society, whether in Uganda or the U.S.A. Addressing this issue requires community-based interventions, stronger support systems, and a renewed focus on fostering healthy, stable family structures.

Fatherhood holds immense power to nurture, shape, and protect, yet when that power is absent or misused, it leaves scars that linger for generations. While understanding God's design for fatherhood brings hope, the reality of father wounds reveals the emotional and psychological impact of a strained or absent father-child relationship. In the next chapter, I explain how these wounds manifest and how to acknowledge them, heal them, and find restoration through God's love.

> *"Fatherlessness is the most destructive trend today."*
> -Dr. Myles Munroe.

CHAPTER EIGHT

THE FATHER WOUND

"An earthly father, as flawed as he may be, is called to reflect the love and wisdom of the Heavenly Father."
– C.S. Lewis.

Fathers play an integral role in shaping their children's identity, self-esteem, and emotional well-being. When the relationship between a father and his child is strained or absent, it can leave deep and lasting wounds, referred to as father wounds, that manifest in various aspects of life. These wounds often stem from absent fathers, emotionally unavailable fathers, or harsh and critical parenting styles. Their impact ripples through a woman or man's life, influencing identity, relationships, and personal fulfillment. This chapter delves into the nature of father wounds in men and women, the behaviors and challenges they create, and the journey toward healing and restoration.

Understanding Father Wounds in Men

A father wound is the emotional or psychological impact caused by a damaged or nonexistent relationship with one's father. Fathers are often viewed as role models, protectors, and sources of validation. When these roles are unfulfilled, the void left behind creates feelings of rejection, abandonment, and insecurity.

For many men, this wound manifests as a sense of incompleteness, driving them to overcompensate through success or retreat into emotional withdrawal. The absence of paternal affirmation leaves men searching for validation in external achievements, relationships, or material possessions, often without finding true fulfillment.

Characteristics of Men with Father Wounds

The effects of father wounds are unique to everyone but often exhibit recurring patterns of behavior and emotional struggles.

Identity Crisis and Insecurity

Without a father's affirmation growing up, men may struggle to define their identity, leading to chronic insecurity. They often seek external validation through career achievements, wealth, or relationships to fill the void left by the absence of a father's guidance.

Fear of Failure and Perfectionism

Driven by an unspoken need to prove their worth, men with father wounds may fear failure and develop perfectionist tendencies. They push themselves to excel yet often feel their efforts are never enough, leading to anxiety, burnout, and a sense of inadequacy.

Difficulty Trusting Authority

Men who had harsh or neglectful fathers growing up may distrust authority figures, seeing them as oppressive or unreliable. Others may seek constant approval from authority figures, yearning for the validation they lacked during childhood.

Emotional Disconnection and Anger

Many men with father wounds struggle to express emotions, leading to emotional disconnection from loved ones. This suppression often hides unresolved anger or resentment, which can result in outbursts or withdrawal from meaningful relationships.

Abusive Behavior toward Women

Some men with unresolved father wounds exhibit abusive or controlling behaviors in relationships. Without a positive model of masculinity, they may resort to aggression or dominance, often as a coping mechanism for insecurity or unresolved pain. I have encountered some of these individuals and endured their actions.

Struggles with Masculinity and Fatherhood

Men who grew up without a father's guidance may question their masculinity or fear repeating their father's mistakes. This can lead to avoidance of fatherhood or difficulty forming strong emotional bonds with their children.

Addictions or Escapism

To numb the pain of father wounds, some men turn to substance abuse, work holism, or escapist behaviors. These coping mechanisms offer temporary relief but often deepen emotional turmoil and hinder healing.

Healing Father Wounds: Steps Toward Restoration

While father wounds leave lasting impressions, healing is possible through intentional efforts, vulnerability, and support.

Acknowledge the Wound

The healing journey begins with acknowledgment. Denying the impact of a father's absence or inadequacy only perpetuates the pain. Recognizing the wound allows men to confront their feelings and take the first step toward emotional restoration.

Seek Counseling or Therapy

Professional counseling or therapy provides a safe space to explore unresolved trauma. Therapists specializing in childhood wounds or Christian counseling can help men address their pain, develop healthy coping strategies, and reconnect with their inner selves.

Embrace God as the Ultimate Father.

For those of faith, God's unconditional love offers a source of healing and affirmation. As the perfect Father, God fills the void left by earthly fathers, offering love, acceptance, and guidance.

Forgive and Release

Forgiveness is a critical step in healing. While it may be challenging, forgiving a father for his absence, neglect, or mistakes releases the emotional hold of resentment and bitterness. Forgiveness does not condone wrong actions but empowers individuals to move forward peacefully.

Build Healthy Relationships

Surrounding oneself with supportive mentors, peers, or spiritual fathers can provide the guidance and affirmation that was lacking. Meaningful relationships offer a foundation for emotional growth and the opportunity to learn from others' wisdom and experiences.

Redefine Masculinity

True masculinity is not defined by societal pressures to appear tough or stoic. It involves vulnerability, love, and care. Redefining masculinity allows men to embrace their full potential, free from harmful stereotypes.

Become the Father You Wish You Had

For men who become fathers, choosing to be present, loving, and nurturing creates a healing path. They build a legacy of affirmation and security for their children by breaking the cycle of father wounds.

Embracing Healing and Redemption

Father wounds can shape a man's identity, relationships, and emotional well-being, but they do not have to define his future. Through intentional healing, acknowledging the pain, seeking support, and embracing the love of God, men can overcome the scars of father wounds and step into a life of wholeness.

True healing requires patience, vulnerability, and grace, but on the other side of the journey lays freedom: the freedom to be the father, husband, and leader one was meant to be. God's unwavering and unconditional love provides the foundation for restoration, allowing men to find their worth, let go of their past, and create a better future for themselves and their families.

The Father Wound in Women

The bond between a father and daughter is one of the most significant relationships in shaping a woman's identity, self-worth, and emotional well-being. Fathers provide a sense of security, love, and affirmation that helps daughters navigate life confidently. Just like in men, this section examines how father wounds affect women, how these wounds manifest, and the path toward healing and restoration.

A father wound occurs when a father fails to fulfill his role as a source of love, affirmation, and protection. This may happen in various ways:

- Absence: A father may be physically absent due to divorce, abandonment, or death.

- Emotional Unavailability: A father might be present but emotionally distant, disengaged, or overly critical.

- Abuse: Emotional, verbal, or physical abuse can inflict deep emotional scars. A father's affirmation is critical to a daughter's sense of self-worth. Women who lack this often have a void that leads to feelings of insecurity, abandonment, and inadequacy, emotions that often persist into adulthood.

How Father Wounds Manifest in Women

Father wounds often reveal themselves through specific emotional, behavioral, and relational struggles.

Insecurity and Low Self-Worth

Without a father's affirmation, many women internalized the belief that they were unlovable or unworthy of attention and care. This can lead to constant validation-seeking from others, creating a dependence on external approval to feel valued.

Promiscuous Behavior

For some women, unresolved father wounds can manifest as promiscuous behavior. This is not merely a pursuit of physical relationships but often a subconscious attempt to seek the affection, validation, and security absent in their paternal relationship. Understanding this behavior as a response to deep emotional voids emphasizes the need to heal the underlying father wound rather than focus solely on the actions themselves.

Fear of Abandonment

The absence of a father can create a persistent fear of being left behind, particularly in romantic relationships. Women with this fear may cling to unhealthy relationships or sabotage connections due to anxiety about being abandoned.

Difficulty in Romantic Relationships

Wounds caused by fathers can shape how women interact with men. They may gravitate toward emotionally unavailable or abusive partners because such dynamics feel familiar, or they may avoid relationships altogether out of fear of vulnerability.

Overcompensation and Perfectionism

Some women respond to father wounds by striving for perfection in academics, careers, or personal achievements. This drive stems from a subconscious hope that being "enough" will earn them the love and validation they lack, though it often leads to burnout and dissatisfaction.

Emotional Numbness or Suppression

To avoid further pain, some women suppress their emotions, creating a barrier to vulnerability and intimacy. While this defense mechanism protects against hurt, it limits their capacity to experience deep love and connection.

Distrust of Male Authority

Women with father wounds may struggle to trust men in positions of authority, such as spouses, employers, pastors, or mentors. This distrust often stems from their fathers' feelings of betrayal or neglect, making it difficult to build healthy relationships.

Difficulty Relating to God as Father

Many women's relationship with their earthly father shapes their perception of God. If their father was absent or unloving, they may struggle to believe in God's unconditional love, making it challenging to trust or rely on Him fully.

Healing From Father Wounds

Although the effects of father wounds can be profound, they are not insurmountable. With intentional steps and a commitment to healing, women can overcome these challenges and rediscover their sense of worth and identity following the following recommendations.

Acknowledge the Pain

The first step in healing is recognizing the wound. Many women suppress their pain, believing they should have moved on. Confronting the feelings of rejection, hurt, or abandonment allows the healing process to begin.

Seek God's Love and Affirmation

God offers the ultimate source of healing. Unlike earthly fathers, God is perfect in His love, always present and unconditionally affirming through His word. He fills the void left by human failings. Prayer, Scripture meditation, and reflection on God's character can help women find the affirmation they crave.

Forgive and Release

Forgiveness is a vital step in the healing journey. While it may be difficult, forgiving a father for his absence, neglect, or mistakes releases the hold of resentment and bitterness. Forgiveness is not about excusing the harm done but about finding freedom from its weight.

Seek Counseling or Therapy

Professional counseling or therapy offers a safe space to process father wounds. Therapists, particularly those with expertise in childhood trauma, can help women unpack unresolved emotions and develop healthier coping strategies. Christian counseling adds a spiritual dimension to this process, helping women connect their healing journey with God's plan for restoration.

Build Healthy Relationships

Positive, affirming relationships with mentors, friends, or spiritual mothers can provide a lack of support and encouragement. These relationships create a safe space for vulnerability and growth, helping women rebuild trust and rediscover their worth.

Break Unhealthy Cycles

Recognizing and breaking patterns of toxic relationships is essential. Women must learn to identify red flags, set boundaries, and seek partners and friends who honor and respect them. By valuing themselves, they can attract healthier connections.

Embrace Your God-Given Identity

Healing involves rediscovering one's identity as a beloved daughter of God. Women are made in God's image, with inherent worth and value that is not dependent on external validation. Embracing this truth fosters confidence and resilience.

Overcome Addictions and Harmful Coping Mechanisms

For some women, unresolved father wounds lead to harmful behaviors, such as substance abuse or settling for abusive relationships. Healing requires the courage to confront these patterns, often with the help of counseling, recovery programs, and spiritual support.

Conclusion: Stepping Into Wholeness

Healing from father wounds is a journey that requires courage, patience, and faith. While the scars of an absent or unloving father may run deep, they do not define a woman's worth or potential. Women can achieve freedom and fulfillment by seeking God's love, building healthy relationships, and confronting emotional pain.

God's perfect love offers the ultimate restoration. As the ultimate Father, He affirms, loves, and nurtures unconditionally, filling the gaps left by earthly fathers. Through Him, women can find healing, reclaim their identity, and embrace a future marked by confidence, wholeness, and love.

Healing from the wounds left by an absent or emotionally detached father is a long and complex process. However, amidst the pain, God often provides figures that unknowingly fill the gap, offering guidance, wisdom, and love. These fatherhood models come in many forms: spiritual leaders, mentors, or friends whose lives reflect the kind of character, integrity, and presence God designed for fathers. I honor the men who stepped into my life and became examples of what fatherhood should look like, inspiring me to hope for a better future.

> *"Age does not cure fatherlessness."*
> -Dr. Myles Munroe

CHAPTER NINE

MY FATHERHOOD MODELS

The greatest thing a father can do for his children is to instill in them a deep love for God."
– Charles Stanley

I have been so blessed even when it has not been direct; some people have fathered me without my conscious awareness. I am most thankful to God for bringing me to a church with over 52 nations represented, which has exposed me to learning about different cultures and backgrounds. Yet, we all come together to worship King Jesus! I have met incredible people who speak into my life, pray for me, and continually check in on my well-being.

I am especially thankful to our lead pastors, Josh and Stephanie, for their leadership. Thank you for obeying God and allowing Him to use you! A special thanks to Pastor Josh, who has preached me into this place! Your teaching, preaching, and authenticity have continually encouraged me **to dream big and live bold**: to act on God's word. **Every Sunday, you preach; know there is a Ugandan girl whose dreams you stretch every time you speak. You've pushed me out of my comfort zone and away from pity parties! You bring me so much courage, hope, and faith!** Above all, I am thankful for the healing I have experienced in this place that gathers all people, no matter their background. I felt broken and ashamed when I first came, but God has healed my heart and dealt with me bountifully through All People Church.

When God spoke to me about joining my current church, I was so afraid because I do not like change! It took me years to make the move, and my greatest frustrations in adult life happened during the season I hesitated. After asking God for His affirmation, He said, **"I will introduce you myself."** Like a crawling baby, I walked into this big church, not knowing what to expect; I just knew I wanted a different future for my children. After a short time of attending, I could tell that God was indeed introducing me.

Amidst so many transitions in this season, I lost my dad and many people in the Ugandan community, and my church were so supportive both financially and emotionally. I am forever thankful to each one who stood with me in that very trying time. Above all, through the Word and a church filled with incredible pastors, partners, and people, I especially identified with one, Pastor Tom Kiessling, in that season.

I remember the very first Sunday I attended after my dad passed away. Pastor Tom preached a sermon titled "The Blessed Hope," which was so comforting and timely! It just confirmed to me that God sees me and that I was in the right place. Over the years, Pastor Tom has consistently brought a word from heaven designed just for me. He has recognized the calling of God upon my life, given me opportunities to serve, and continually encouraged me.

Someone in a meeting with him once texted me, saying, *"Vivienne, just know Pastor Tom delights in you; his face lights up when he talks about you. He is so proud of you!"* That truly touched me. God has shown His love for me through Pastor Tom, who has continually been a blessing, especially when he shared a pertinent story concerning fatherhood on my show, Conversations That Edify, at Photizo Daily.

I think his life and experience as a husband and a father are models that some of us need. Ladies and gentlemen, I believe his sharing about Fatherhood will help you, if you have the same struggles as I did.

Pastor Tom: *I am a father of three adult kids, two of whom are married, and I have two grandchildren. Fatherhood has been a real joyful experience for me. I believe it starts with having the right foundation in your life. Cheryl and I had a good courtship, received premarital counseling, and learned about marriage and the roles God gives us, and that became the foundation of being a good father.*

We had a one-and-a-half-year engagement, living together as a couple, learning to communicate, building agreements, and living life together. After four years of marriage, we had our first child, Lauren. Melissa was born Four years later, and Brian was born four years after that. Cheryl and I have had the joy as both mum and dad of going through the seasons of life with our children. There are different seasons in a family.

In the early years, when the children were still toddlers and young, I learned a lot from Cheryl; she is a nurturer with a large capacity to give, nurture, care, listen, and understand. I was not raised that way, as I grew up in a slightly different environment; I tended to bark (raise my voice). So, I learned that was not the way to nurture and raise children. I learned to listen, observe, watch, and understand the beautiful gifts God had placed in my life, my children.

Just as mothers naturally bond with their children, dads also need to bond with their kids at an early age by providing lots of nurture. It takes a secure man to nurture. Nurture is not a womanly quality; God Himself is a nurturer, He nurtures us, He affirms us, He believes in us. Children need to hear the voices of their fathers affirm them. Fathers need to affirm their children.

Young girls need to feel loved, cared for, and protected by their dads, and sons need to know that their dads believe in them, respect them, and honor them. This comes through how we listen and speak to our children. You see it often at grocery stores when some yell at their children. Yelling does not work. You must be patient and understand the seasons of your children's lives. Children do not subscribe to your convenience; you must be spontaneous. As fathers, we need to engage with our children. A lot of fathers do not know how to play. Play with them, and create a fun, joyful atmosphere that enables children to be as open as God created them to be.

Cheryl and I were blessed to establish an environment where the Spirit of God dwelt in our home. Anyone who visited our home would experience the peace and joy present there. Fathers are responsible for creating that atmosphere in their homes. One valuable habit was having regular family dinners, where we sat down and talked about everything. We turned off devices and focused on spending time together. This was especially important during the preteen and teen years.

Even amidst ministry demands, I prioritized being home for family dinner. That is a practical thing you can do; you must be present. Being present in every season of your children's lives is crucial; if you aren't, you will look back with regret in later years. When you invest in your children, that love, honor, care, and respect will be reciprocated by you in the later years.

Seeing our children grow into healthy, successful adults has brought us great joy. They relate well to authority and their peers and have Christ-centered relationships. This is the fruit of creating a nurturing environment from the start. Teaching our children responsibility was also important, even though it required constant repetition. As fathers, we must be models and examples to our children.

To be a good father means you must also be a good husband. Caring for your wife teaches you how to care for your children. I remember Cheryl and I in the kitchen after dinner, showing affection to each other, and our children would squeeze between us for a big family hug and huddle. Touch is important. In some cultures, people may be stand-off-ish or nonverbal and may not be high touch, but Jesus was verbal and high touch. Our touch is a touch of affirmation. Children need that affirmation and warm touch.

As fathers, we are responsible for leading our families. Unfortunately, some dads become passive, but leadership at home starts with fathers. For us, going to church was non-negotiable; it came before sports or anything else. Dads must lead their families to church. They must be more proactive in their role. Family dinner, church, and outreach were our priorities. Fatherhood has brought me great fulfillment, and there is no greater joy than seeing your children work out of the values you've taught them. Being present in their lives, whether as toddlers, preteens, or young adults, is the most important thing you can do. Fatherhood is a joy, and it should be nothing less.

Vivienne: Thank you so much, Pastor. I remember where I come from: some fathers come home, the kids disappear, and even some wives! Hahaha. Can you please speak about the essence of parents speaking into their children's lives? Especially in African culture, parents often feel their responsibility ends with providing school fees and material needs. They say, "I paid for everything; what more do you want from me?" Can you emphasize the need for affirmation?

Pastor Tom: *"Absolutely, Vivienne. Let us start by looking at the scripture in Deuteronomy 6:4-5. God gave parents, both moms and dads, a mandate to raise godly children who love the Lord. There are two components to this mandate. First, as parents, we need to be passionate about the things of God. That passion flows into everything else we do. If mom and dad aren't passionate about Jesus or doing things God's way, it won't transfer to the next generation.*

Second, in that same passage, God commands Israel to talk about His Word in every aspect of daily life when you're on the way, rise, and go to sleep. In other words, parents must always be on call and ready to speak about life to their children. Do not be rigid or put your kids in a box. They have their journey with God, and you are there to facilitate that. This begins by adopting the mandate God has given parents: to lead the way, be passionate for Him, and speak into their children's lives.

It is not about beating them repeatedly with, "You should do this because the Bible says so." It is about affirming them, letting them know that God loves them, cares for them, has a future for them, and has entrusted them into your care. As parents, we need to model and be examples for our children. That means nurturing them and providing correction, when necessary, but correction shouldn't come through yelling, verbal abuse, or even physical abuse. That's not right. I followed a formula when raising my kids through the different seasons of life: they need 90% nurture and 10% correction.

If you provide the nurture they need, you won't have to correct them that often because they feel safe, loved, and open to sharing with you. When they make a mistake, they won't expect you to explode but rather to use it as a coaching moment. At the same time, you can reaffirm that you love, are proud of, and believe in them.

Even Jesus needed affirmation. Before He began His ministry and faced the devil in the wilderness, the Father spoke at His baptism, saying, "This is my Son, in whom I am well pleased." Children need to know, "Does Daddy love me? Is he pleased with me? Does he believe in me?" They might not say these things, but they are thinking about them in their hearts. This is what I call the spiritual bond parents have with their children.

Your responsibility goes beyond providing money and a safe place to live. You're responsible for creating a safe emotional space where they can open up, have conversations, and develop a deep bond of friendship. That friendship will evolve, but you are a steward of a beautiful gift God has given you right now. Recognizing that your responsibility is more than just putting a roof over their heads is important. You are called to emulate Jesus Christ to them, to show them the love of God.

When children look at their parents, they see a divine authority. If they see their father as abusive, they will think God is abusive because that's their reference point. We need to be models and examples. As I said before, we must be present in their lives spiritually, emotionally, and not just financially. Providing for your kids is good, but protecting, preparing them for the future, and speaking into their lives lies with us as dads.

When you come home exhausted at the end of the day, the real work begins. Engage in conversation with your children; do not lock yourself in a room or disconnect. Do not just turn on the TV and zone out. These are golden opportunities to build relationships that will pay off in later years."

Vivienne: "Thank you so much, Pastor! Do men have to prepare to be fathers? Also, what have you passed on to your children that they have passed on to their grandchildren?"

Pastor Tom: "Not preparing for fatherhood is like jumping off a diving board into deep waters; you learn as you go. There are great resources, like James Dobson's Focus on the Family and Jimmy and Karen Evans' XO Marriage podcast, which can help you get an education on fatherhood. The onus is on men to educate themselves. When buying a house or choosing a career, we research and prepare. But with marriage and family, many roll into it, and it is often a baptism of fire. So yes, preparation through knowledge is important, but real learning begins when you become a father.

Fatherhood is a collaborative effort with your wife. Wives have a unique perspective, and it is wise to allow them to make decisions in parenting actively. As men, we often have a narrow view, but when married to a godly woman, it removes the blinders and provides a broader perspective. Across cultures, many men say, "I know what to do, do not tell me." But that's a lack of wisdom. Men need to be secure. Secure men allow their wives to stand shoulder to shoulder with them and give them counsel on how to raise children. Seeking counsel from your wife and learning as you walk through the different seasons of parenthood is crucial.

I'm a big advocate for continual learning. I'm going to be 65, and I'm still learning. Having a teachable attitude, humility, and recognizing that there is always room for improvement is vital. I have seen older men get stuck in their ways, and that's not where you want to be.

What I have passed down to my children is a passion for Jesus, a passion for family because family is a lifestyle for us, and a value of being part of the church. The church is God's design, and being plugged into a local church is essential for fulfilling His plan for your life. Our kids have embraced these values, and they're all engaged in their local churches.

We've also passed down the concept of honor, which is learning to relate well with others. Each of our kids is uniquely gifted, whether more introverted or extroverted, but regardless of their personalities, they have a passion for God and people. Being compassionate and understanding is important, especially in a culture that opposes the gospel. We are not judgmental; instead, we engage in friendship, reflecting how Jesus was a friend of sinners."

Vivienne: "Thank you so much for sharing, Pastor! On this Father's Day, we hear about the increasing trend of fatherlessness. What do you say about the effects of absentee fathers in our generation?"

Pastor Tom: *"Fatherlessness is a huge issue today. I have ministered to men in prison, and what you see firsthand is how broken relationships with their fathers have led to criminal behavior, drug abuse, and deep emotional wounds. Many of these men, though robust, have cried during ministry, reflecting* the pain caused by absent or abusive fathers. The Bible says that if fathers do not turn their hearts back to their children, there will be a curse upon the land, and we see that curse today.

One major contributor to fatherlessness is pornography. It is devastating to marriages and families, and statistics show no difference between Christian men and others when it comes to this addiction. Pornography destroys a man's ability to relate properly to women and often leads to neglect and abuse. Other addictions, like alcohol, can follow, further compounding the problem. The only solution is repentance and accountability. We need to reach men with the gospel, not to shame or emasculate them, but to offer forgiveness and restoration.

Just like Jesus offered mercy to the woman caught in adultery, fathers can be restored if they come to a place of repentance. It is not easy, especially when trust has been broken, but healing starts with taking accountability and seeking help. A strong devotional life is essential, as I have seen men trapped in these cycles often have no connection with God. Surrounding yourself with godly men who lead well and know how to parent is also crucial for healing. God's heart is not to judge but to heal and restore. Fathers who have been absent or abusive can find healing through repentance and by re-establishing a connection with God and with others who can walk the journey of restoration with them."

Vivienne: "It is heartbreaking to hear about the impact of fatherlessness. How does someone break away from the pain of never knowing their father or being estranged from their children?"

Pastor Tom: *"It is incredibly hard, Vivienne. Time may help heal some wounds, but the scars of losing a father or being separated from your children never fully disappear. The pain of that void will always be there. But the best way to deal with it is by drawing near to the Lord and experiencing the love of the*

Father. The Bible says to cast all your cares upon Him because He cares for you. The Father's love is often distorted in our culture, but God is not distant or judgmental. He delights in showing mercy. The prophet Micah says, "I do not delight in the punishment of the wicked, but I delight in mercy and compassion."

The scar of loss may remain, but the presence of God, through the Holy Spirit, brings comfort and healing. Jesus is referred to as the balm of Gilead, and He is the one who soothes the deepest wounds. Even when the memory of loss is still there, you can go to your heavenly Father. He hears our complaints, our cries, and our sorrow. Just as David encouraged himself in the Lord during his trials, we, too, can find solace in God's presence. Letting God's love fill the void is the first step toward healing from the deep pain of fatherlessness."

Positive fatherhood models in my life have been a blessing I will forever appreciate. These men provided glimpses of what true fatherhood could be, yet their influence could not fully erase the wounds left behind. It became clear that unaddressed pain from childhood still lingered beneath the surface, shaping my identity and relationships. Join me in confronting the roots of that trauma and its long-lasting effects.

> "The most important thing a father can do for his children is to love their mother."
> —Dr. Myles Munroe

CHAPTER TEN

CHILDHOOD TRAUMA

"The heart of a father is the masterpiece of nature."
– Antoine François Prévost

Many of us struggle in relationships, marriages, workplaces, and other aspects of life, often unaware that the root of our frustrations lies in unresolved childhood trauma. Blaming others or external circumstances is easier, but true growth requires introspection. Without addressing these wounds, we risk perpetuating cycles of pain, projecting our insecurities onto others, and making decisions driven by fear or desperation. I hope and pray that after reading this book, we will take responsibility for our trauma and embrace the courage to share our experiences openly rather than hiding them, especially when forming new relationships.

Recognizing the Ripple Effect of Unhealed Trauma

Our unresolved trauma influences how we approach life and relationships. I have seen this firsthand. For instance, a close friend of mine walked away from a seven-year friendship because I did not meet their unrealistic expectations. Knowing their background and the challenges they faced growing up, I recognized they were struggling with childhood trauma. Though hurt, I chose patience and empathy, understanding that unresolved pain often manifests in ways even the person experiencing it may not fully understand.

Still, as much as trauma may explain our behavior, it does not absolve us of responsibility. We owe it to ourselves and those around us to reflect, seek healing, and break free from the patterns that bind us. Living in self-pity or burdening others without addressing the root of our pain only perpetuates the cycle.

Taking Responsibility

Once, I was with friends waiting for someone who failed to show up without communication. A friend attributed his behavior to unresolved childhood issues. While that might be true, I reminded them that the world does not pause for our trauma. Regardless of our past, we are accountable for our present actions.

Trauma can affect how we respond to seemingly simple situations. For example, my sister refuses to let her child spend a night in the village because of memories from our childhood. My mother, unable to comprehend, often asks, "What was so bad?" While I do not recall anything significant enough to justify this fear, even minor unresolved incidents like my neglected dental health, shape how I plan to parent. Trauma does not need to be monumental to have a lasting impact.

What Is Childhood Trauma?

Childhood trauma refers to experiences that cause intense physical, emotional, or psychological distress, overwhelming a child's ability to cope. These events leave lasting effects on development, well-being, and adult functioning.

Sources of Childhood Trauma
- Abuse: Physical, verbal, emotional, or sexual harm.
- Neglect: Failing to meet a child's basic needs.
- Family Dysfunction: Exposure to domestic violence, substance abuse, or severe conflict.
- Loss or Separation: Death of or prolonged separation from a parent or caregiver.
- Bullying: Persistent harassment by peers
- Natural Disasters or Accidents: Witnessing or experiencing catastrophic events.
- Community Violence: Exposure to gang violence, shootings, or riots.

Personal Encounters with Trauma

Trauma often hides in plain sight, influencing our reactions subtly yet profoundly. I recall meeting someone who brought joy and meaningful conversations into my life. When their circumstances changed, they had to shift priorities. While I logically understood, emotionally, I felt abandoned.

Instead of processing the situation rationally, my unresolved trauma took control, causing me to act out, withdraw, and feel rejected. Their eventual confrontation forced me to admit that my behavior was rooted in a fear of abandonment. For them, it was not rejection, but for me, my past was projecting itself onto the present.

This realization was both freeing and sobering. While being open helped, I also learned that managing my emotions is ultimately my responsibility. Not everyone can understand or accommodate my triggers, nor should they have to. Whether they just wanted to stop dealing with me or not, my reaction did not need to be that way. It shouldn't have affected me so deeply; I should have let them go without drama. Everyone has the right to build or leave relationships.

The Long-Term Impact of Childhood Trauma

Unresolved trauma manifests in ways that shape every aspect of our lives:

Emotional and Mental Health

Anxiety: A constant state of worry, often tied to fear of reliving past pain.
Depression: Feelings of hopelessness stemming from unresolved emotional wounds.

Behavioral Issues

Difficulty forming or maintaining relationships due to trust issues and fear of vulnerability. Acting out, either through rebellion or excessive people-pleasing.

Distorted Self-Image

Internalized feelings of inadequacy often lead to perfectionism or overcompensation.

Physical Health Challenges

Chronic stress from trauma can lead to long-term health problems, such as cardiovascular issues or weakened immune systems.

Choosing Healing

Understanding my past has profoundly shaped how I approach people and situations. It has taught me to extend grace, knowing that many behaviors stem not from malice but from unresolved wounds. Trauma is not an excuse but a context, a lens through which we can better understand ourselves and others.

Healing begins with acknowledgment. It is about facing pain, seeking support, and intentionally choosing to rewrite the narratives that once held us captive. While the process may be uncomfortable, it is the first step toward freedom, healthier relationships, and a more fulfilling life.

Recovering from Childhood Trauma

Childhood trauma can leave deep wounds on the soul, often lingering into adulthood, shaping our thoughts, behaviors, and even our relationship with God. As Christians, we believe in the transformative power of Christ's love and healing, yet the recovery process can be challenging. Together, let us explore how to navigate the journey of healing from childhood trauma through faith, scripture, and practical steps rooted in Christian principles.

Acknowledging the Pain

The first step in healing is acknowledging the pain. Many believers struggle with admitting their hurt, feeling that it may indicate a lack of faith or trust in God. However, the Bible encourages us to bring our burdens to the Lord.

In Psalm 34:18, it is written, *"The Lord is close to the brokenhearted and saves those who are crushed in spirit."* Recognizing and admitting the pain is not a sign of weakness but rather a step toward inviting God into the deepest parts of our hearts.

Understanding God's Compassion

One of the most comforting aspects of our faith is knowing that God understands our suffering. Hebrews 4:15(NIV) reminds us, *"For we do not have a high priest who is unable to empathize with our weaknesses, but we have one who has been tempted in every way, just as we are, yet he did not sin."*

Jesus, who endured betrayal, loneliness, and pain, fully understands the depth of human suffering. His compassion is endless, and He is always ready to walk us through our healing process.

Forgiveness and Reconciliation

Forgiveness is a powerful step in the journey of healing. It does not mean condoning the wrongs done to us but rather releasing the past's hold on our present and future. Jesus spoke about forgiveness extensively, highlighting its importance in our spiritual and emotional well-being. Matthew 6:14-15NIVsays, *"For if you forgive other people when they sin against you, your heavenly Father will also forgive you. But your father will not forgive your sins if you do not forgive others."*

I initially felt offended when Pastor Fredrick preached to us in 2018, but I realized it was the word cutting deep into my heart. It took me time to act on it, but I knew God was speaking to me. I have since met many others who struggle in their relationships, especially with their parents or guardians. Here's the truth: God wants to heal us; there is nothing too big for God to heal and forgive.

He calls us to be free from pain, anger, and bitterness. Release it all to Him. Forgiving those who have caused us trauma can be incredibly difficult, but it is essential for our healing. It allows us to break free from the cycle of pain and bitterness, opening the door for God's peace to enter our hearts. Forgiving ourselves for guilt or shame is also important, as God's grace covers all.

Renewing the Mind

Childhood trauma often leaves lasting imprints on the mind, shaping our thoughts and beliefs about ourselves, others, and even God. The Apostle Paul encourages us to renew our minds in Romans 12:2 NIV: *"Do not conform to the pattern of this world but be transformed by renewing your mind. Then you will be able to test and approve what God's will is: his good, pleasing, and perfect will."*

Renewing the mind involves replacing the lies that trauma has ingrained in us with the truth of God's Word. It requires consistent prayer, meditation on scripture, and sometimes professional counseling to help us realign our thoughts with God's promises.

Embracing God's Identity for You

Trauma often distorts our identity, making us believe that we are unworthy, unlovable, or damaged. However, the Bible is clear about who we are in Christ. 2 Corinthians 5:17(NLT) tells us "That *anyone who belongs to Christ has become a new person. The old life is gone; a new life has begun!"* Embracing this new identity is crucial in the healing process.

Walking with Christ, we learn to see ourselves through His eyes. We are no longer defined by our past or our trauma but by God's love and grace. This new identity empowers us to live in freedom and purpose, fully aligned with God's life plan.

Community and Support

God designed us to live in a community, and healing is often facilitated through the support of others. The church, counselors, and trusted friends can provide a safe space for sharing, processing, and healing. My church, which has been so significant in my healing, often encourages us not to do life alone. One of our core values says, "Community is our design."

In the Christian community, we find people who will pray with us, encourage us, and remind us of God's truths when we struggle to believe them ourselves. The healing journey is not meant to be walked alone, and God often uses others to be His hands and feet in our lives.

The Power of Prayer and Worship

Prayer and worship are powerful tools in the healing process. When we pray, we communicate directly with God, pouring out our hearts and inviting His healing presence into our wounds. We should surrender our pain to God as soon as we acknowledge it.

Philippians 4:6-7(NIV) encourages us, "Do not be anxious about anything, but in every situation, by prayer and petition, with thanksgiving, present your requests to God. And the peace of God, which transcends all understanding, will guard your hearts and your minds in Christ Jesus."

I think sometimes we underrate worship, but it is so powerful. Worship shifts our focus from our pain to God's greatness. It reminds us of His sovereignty, love, and healing power. In moments of worship, we often experience a deep connection with God, where His peace and comfort flood our souls, bringing healing in ways that words cannot describe.

Honor your Parents

Honoring abusive parents is a delicate and complex matter that requires wisdom, grace, and discernment. The Bible's command to honor parents does not mean enduring abuse or neglecting your well-being. Instead, it calls you to approach the situation with a heart of forgiveness, setting healthy boundaries, seeking healing, and trusting God's justice.

Honoring an abusive parent may look different from traditional expressions of respect and care. It could mean praying for them, seeking God's will for their life, or simply refraining from speaking ill of them. Romans 12:17-19 NIV says, *"Do not repay anyone evil for evil. Be careful to do what is right in the eyes of everyone. If possible, as it depends on you, live at peace with everyone. Do not take revenge, my dear friends, but leave room for God's wrath, for it is written: 'It is mine to avenge; I will repay,' says the Lord."*

This passage highlights the importance of leaving justice in God's hands while striving to live peacefully. You can honor your parents by choosing not to repay their harm with harm but instead trusting God to bring justice and healing in His time. God is just.

Parents, Do Not Provoke Your Children

"Fathers, do not provoke your children to anger, but bring them up in the discipline and instruction of the Lord."
- Ephesians 6:4 (ESV)

Exasperation refers to the intense frustration or anger children experience when pushed beyond their emotional limits. It stems from parenting missteps, such as unreasonable expectations, which hold children to impossible standards; inconsistent discipline and overly changing rules that leave children confused and insecure; lack of empathy, dismissing or invalidating their feelings; overprotection, stifling their independence; and favoritism, creating jealousy and resentment among siblings. These behaviors create emotional wounds that can profoundly affect a child's development and their relationship with their parents.

While much focus is placed on children's behavior, we rarely address how parents can provoke their children. Cultural norms often discourage addressing an elder's mistakes, but even the Bible instructs parents not to provoke their children. Reflecting on personal experiences, I have seen how such provocation can shape a child's outlook and actions.

A Lesson in Communication

I recall feeling frustrated with my father for failing to meet my needs without explanation. Exhausted by the pattern, I blocked him. A teenager blocking their father may seem extreme, but it became my coping mechanism. Years later, when my mom asked about someone else, I had blocked, she said, "What if God blocked you for everything you've done?" Her words cut deep, reminding me of the importance of forgiveness and reconciliation. Still, I realized that unresolved conflict had taught me avoidance rather than resolution, a skill I had to learn as an adult. Blocking people now serves my peace, not my anger.

Misplaced Expectations

On my 24th birthday, I brought home cake from my church family, grateful for their kindness. Yet, before I could share the joy, my mother remarked, "At your age, you can't even get someone to give you a birthday cake and presents?" Her words stung. Was I supposed to feel inadequate for not having any special person celebrating with me? Hurt, I chose not to share the cake with my family, taking it to my colleagues at work instead. Statements like these, often normalized in African parenting, drive many children to seek validation elsewhere in relationships, substance abuse, or even destructive behaviors.

Struggles after School

After finishing college, I faced challenges that tested my resilience. Without financial support from my mother, I missed opportunities and felt trapped in my grandmother's house. Depression, though not recognized at the time, took hold, leaving me unmotivated and overwhelmed.

One incident stands out: My mother scolded me for buying a more expensive item than she had requested. The emotional weight of her reaction, combined with my financial struggles, deepened my resentment of staying home. I remember spending a whole week thinking about where to go but couldn't because I was flat broke.

Conversations with great friends like Derrick, who said, "Two tigers cannot live on the same hill," have helped me navigate many difficult periods because I would have surely fallen out with my mom so many times. Some days were worse than others!

Emotional Dismissal

As I have matured, my relationship with my mother has evolved. Once merely my provider, she's become someone I seek emotional support from. However, not all attempts have been successful. One day, I sought her advice about troubling patterns in my life. Her response?

"When something fails, just ignore it and move on to another thing!" Though practical, it was not the comfort I needed. Instead, I felt dismissed.

This experience reinforced the need for parents to meet their children with empathy, not just solutions. When someone seeks comfort, they do not want quick fixes; they need listening, understanding, and reassurance.

One cold Sunday evening, while driving through downtown Boston, I saw a sign for a psychic in one of the shops. Though I did not know much about it, I had heard a preacher talk about such people. I felt a sudden urge to go there and discover what was wrong with me, which patterns I had asked my mom, and she dismissed. The devil offered a fleeting solution in that moment of vulnerability, but I was also hesitant.

Someone may ask, what about the Holy Spirit? When you're emotionally devastated, it can be difficult to tell or even yield to His voice amidst the chaos of overwhelming thoughts. Thankfully, I recognized it as a trap, chose to avoid it, and turned to prayer instead, reaffirming the importance of spiritual grounding in times of vulnerability. I am sure it is the Holy Spirit that helped me not go. It is important to quiet our spirits so we can always hear His voice, but I can't deny that sometimes, you truly need counsel from trusted people.

The Role of Parents in Shaping Children's Futures

Parental words and actions leave lasting impressions. Stories of abuse and neglect are rampant: parents introducing immorality through their language, behaviors, or media choices, openly engaging in substance abuse before their children, and fathers neglecting their responsibilities. These actions create cycles of dysfunction in children.

For example, I met another senior citizen who started drinking alcohol at age seven because his father kept liquor at their disposal. Another friend admitted that his mother's smoking influenced his descent into substance abuse until he met me, someone who inspired him to change. These stories highlight how parental choices directly impact children's behavior and future decisions.

The Consequences of Neglect

Provision is a fundamental responsibility. What options are left when parents refuse to meet their children's basic needs? In Uganda, I have seen firsthand how parental neglect pushes children toward prostitution, early marriages, child labor, drug abuse, robbery, and even witchcraft. While parents may not explicitly condone these actions, their neglect and harsh words often drive children to such extremes.

> "It is the influence I have on them, seeing them do what I do! Even the baby, when I'm in church, raising my hands, does the same thing!"
> —Carmelo A. at Photizo Daily

Breaking the Cycle

Parents, your actions and words matter deeply. Anger, selfishness, and neglect create wounds that children carry into adulthood. It is time to break these cycles. Speak life, not destruction. Teach kindness, humility, and grace. Recognize that your role isn't just to provide but to nurture, guide, and affirm.

The Bible instructs us to "Speak grace to others." As parents, let us embody this principle, creating environments where children feel loved, valued, and supported. By doing so, we can help them grow into resilient, compassionate individuals, free from the weight of generational pain.

Conclusion: Trusting in God's Process

Healing from childhood trauma is a journey, one that requires patience, faith, and persistence. There will be days of progress and may be relapses for some, but through it all, God is faithful. These scriptures should encourage us to put our trust in God.

Isaiah 43:2-3(NLT): *I will be with you when you go through deep waters. When you go through rivers of difficulty, you will not drown. When you walk through the fire of oppression, you will not be burned up.*

Psalms 147:3(NIV) says *He heals the brokenhearted and binds up their wounds.*

As we trust in God's process, we can rest assured that He is with us, working all things together for our good. God knows every tear, every prayer, every step toward forgiveness and renewal, and will complete the work He has begun in us. Through His grace, God wants us to emerge from the shadows of our past into the glorious light of His healing and love. Amen

Childhood trauma leaves wounds that can take years to heal, shaping the way we see ourselves and others. Yet, amidst this pain, women, men, mothers, sisters, and caregivers often step in to nurture and love with unmatched strength and resilience. Let us honor the mothers and ladies whose sacrifices, presence, and unwavering support help mend broken pieces and provide hope where fathers may have been absent.

VIVIENNE D'AMOUR

*"It is pure joy when I come home, and they welcome me back from work. Their innocence is everything!
I could have a bad day at work but knowing I'm going home to have my beautiful baby boys is enough."*
–Carmelo A. at Photizo Daily

CHAPTER ELEVEN

MOTHERS/LADIES

"To her, the name of father was another name for love."
– Fanny Fern

When an acquaintance asked why I focus so much on fatherlessness, I shared that it's part of my assignment to unmask the effects of fatherlessness and, from personal experience, to continue highlighting the significance of fathers in children's lives. Mothers, by default, rarely need reminders about their roles. Yet, many women today dismiss the need for fathers in their children's lives not because these men are inherently unfit but due to the mother's financial independence and sometimes lack of emotional intelligence. This dismissal is often tied to emotional responses, an area where many of us, including myself, struggle.

Navigating Emotions and Their Impact

I have personally battled with emotional abuse, not only in relationships but also through my lack of emotional intelligence. For years, I let anger, despair, and fleeting feelings control my decisions. I have sold myself short, wasted precious time, and found myself in spaces I should have avoided because I allowed emotions to drive me. By God's grace, I have healed and learned to rely on the Holy Spirit when emotions threaten to overwhelm me.

Emotions, while natural, are fleeting and can be deceptive. Think about the times you felt like you could not live without someone, only to wonder later what you were thinking. Or moments of intense anger that faded into insignificance. Many make life-altering decisions based on temporary emotions, failing to realize how fleeting they are.

For example, I have often been asked why I still communicate with people who betrayed or hurt me. My answer is simple: The emotions of hurt have passed. My mother's stories of my father checking on her many years after their separation taught me this truth. The intensity of emotions diminishes over time, yet the bonds of shared experiences, like raising a child together, remain. I urge us to pause before making permanent decisions based on temporary feelings.

Understanding Emotions

Emotions are complex psychological states involving subjective experiences, physiological responses, and expressive behaviors. They shape our decisions, interactions, and self-perception. Instead of suppressing or dismissing them, we should allow ourselves to feel and process them constructively.

Types of Emotions
Basic Emotions. Paul Ekman identifies six universal emotions:
Joy: Triggered by positive experiences, fostering happiness and contentment.
Sadness: A response to loss or disappointment, encouraging reflection and support-seeking.
Fear: Alerts us to danger, prompting protective responses.
Anger: Arises from perceived injustice or frustration, motivating corrective action.

Surprise: Evoked by the unexpected, leading to curiosity or confusion.
Disgust: Protects us from harmful substances or situations.
Complex Emotions: These blends of basic emotions influenced by personal experiences, such as:
Jealousy: A combination of fear, sadness, and anger in relationships.
Guilt: Remorse over violating personal standards.
Shame: A self-conscious response to perceived shortcomings.
Positive vs. Negative Emotions
Positive Emotions: Enhance well-being (e.g., love, gratitude, hope)
Negative Emotions: While uncomfortable, they foster growth when processed (e.g., sadness, anger).

The Role of Emotions

Emotions serve several critical functions:

- Decision-Making: They guide actions in navigating challenges.
- Relationships: Emotions shape connections, fostering bonds or creating conflicts.
- Self-Reflection: They provide insights into personal values, experiences, and needs.

Cultivating Emotional Intelligence

Emotional Intelligence (EI) is recognizing, understanding, and managing emotions while empathizing.

Key components include:
- Self-awareness: Understanding your emotions.
- Self-Regulation: Controlling emotional responses.
- Empathy: Recognizing and understanding others' emotions.
- Social Skills: Building and maintaining healthy relationships.

Ways to Enhance Emotional Intelligence
- Mindfulness: Observe emotions without judgment to improve regulation.
- Journaling: Writing clarifies thoughts and promotes healing.
- Seeking Support: Share emotions with trusted friends, family, or professionals.

Resources for Emotional Growth

Two books that have profoundly shaped my understanding of emotions and relationships are:

Marriage on the Rock by Jimmy Evans; a resource for individuals in all stages of relationships, whether single, married, or divorced. It provides valuable insights for building strong marital foundations.

Emotionally Healthy Spirituality by Peter Scazzero. A guide to integrating emotional and spiritual health, helping readers steady their emotional lives and deepen their spiritual roots.

Understanding and managing emotions is essential for personal growth and thriving relationships. By embracing emotional awareness, we can navigate life's challenges with resilience, fostering deeper connections with others and God. While emotions can be intense and overwhelming, they are not permanent, and with the right tools, we can learn to respond thoughtfully rather than impulsively.

Growth in emotional intelligence and knowledge, especially through resources like these books, equips us to approach relationships and life with clarity and grace.

As Dr. Myles Munroe once said, "Knowledge sustains marriage." I believe it sustains marriage and every meaningful relationship in our lives.

Emotions Mismanaged

The Bible warns us that following the desires of the flesh leads to destruction, which applies to our emotions. As women, we are naturally emotional beings, but we are also called to crucify the flesh and allow the Holy Spirit to guide our decisions. Ask yourself: When you entered that relationship, was it God leading you, or were you following your feelings? When you decided to cut off the father of your child, was it God directing you?

I once conversed with a woman who planned to cut ties with her child's father. I asked her a question she was unprepared for, "Are you ready to be a single mom?". It was not about doubting her strength but encouraging her to reflect deeply. Too often, we make life-altering decisions in the heat of emotional turmoil without praying, seeking wise counsel, or preparing for the realities ahead.

Parenting, especially as a single mother, is no small task. It requires grit, sacrifice, and, above all, divine guidance. Though we may never feel fully prepared for the challenges of raising children, we can build a strong foundation by involving God in every decision.

Financial Stability

While many women today can independently care for their children, it is essential to acknowledge the sacrifices and challenges of this responsibility. Financial stability does not come easily, and the struggle is even harder for those who do not plan, refuse to work, or rely solely on others for support.

It is admirable to take on the responsibility of raising a child alone, but if you claim you do not need the father's support, why resort to resentment or cursing when no one steps in to help? If God led you to that decision, trust Him to provide. One lesson I have learned is that emotions do not pay bills.

I recall speaking to another woman in Uganda who intended to cut off the child's father. When I asked how she planned to support her child financially, she replied, "Vivienne, this isn't America where women work tirelessly to provide." Her response stunned me. While cultural expectations may differ, the responsibility of providing for a child remains universal. Years later, I saw her struggle to find financial help, caught in a cycle of dependency and frustration.

Many women end up in unhealthy relationships due to emotional instability or financial pressure. Do not let fleeting emotions or financial dependence compromise your worth. As someone who has let emotions dictate decisions, I can say it is never worth the pain.

Raising Children

Parenting requires a foundation that goes beyond momentary emotions. The Bible encourages us to "count the cost" before building, I believe it also applies to raising children. The strength of any family lies in its foundation. While parenting is never without challenges, the presence of two parents often provides a more balanced emotional and disciplinary environment, particularly during a child's teenage years. As a single parent of a 3-year-old, have you thought about what it will be like when they reach their adolescent stage? Will they listen to you as they do today?

As a newbie in cybersecurity, I appreciate its critical role in protecting networks, information, and systems. No entity can thrive without proper security measures in place. One aspect I love about ethical hacking is penetration testing, where security professionals simulate attacks to identify vulnerabilities and strengthen defenses. Similarly, I believe parenting operates as a system, and parents must be prepared to guard against risks based on the vulnerabilities within their family dynamics. They should continually educate themselves, conduct assessments to evaluate their parenting approaches and adapt to create a safe and nurturing environment for their children.

Reflecting on my childhood, I now understand the challenges my mom faced raising us alone. As teenagers, my sister and I often found her difficult, but in hindsight, I saw she was doing her best. Without another parent to share the emotional load, she had no one to offer a different perspective, leaving our home full of tension.

Single mothers often feel overwhelmed, juggling sacrifices, discipline, and emotional support. Many break down under these challenges, feeling isolated and unsupported. Parenting is not meant to be done alone, and the absence of a father's emotional balance can create long-term consequences for children.

Even biblical examples emphasize the importance of shared parenting. Mary and Joseph raised Jesus together, demonstrating unity and shared responsibility. When Jesus went missing at 12, they searched for Him together. Though Jesus was about His Heavenly Father's business, His earthly parents were present and concerned.

My mother often reflects on how her parenting approach has evolved, and I love that she has not stopped learning. She continually advocates for parents not to separate from their children. I hope one day we read or hear her story. She is full of wisdom. Wisdom from elders is invaluable. As the Bible teaches us, older women should teach young women to learn to submit to their husbands. We should seek counsel, accountability, and guidance from those who have gone before us. I am praying and hoping we have more senior mothers and wives to arise and speak to the young generation. Please don't keep your experience to yourself; we need it!

Breaking the Cycle

How can we break free from emotional cycles and unhealthy patterns? The answer lies in submission to God, not our emotions.

As women, we often face overwhelming emotional, financial, and relational battles. But true freedom comes when we surrender these struggles to God. For me, breaking free from toxic patterns required surrendering completely. I had to cry out to God, return to His Word, and restore my fellowship with Him.

Some of us do not need another relationship; we need time with God. He understands and heals in ways no one else can. The Bible encourages us to approach Him boldly, seeking mercy and grace. When we submit our emotions to God, the enemy loses his hold over us.

Trust God to lead you; He will provide the strength and clarity to navigate life's challenges. By placing our emotions under His authority, we can make sound decisions that honor Him and create a better future for ourselves and our children.

> "Emotional health and spiritual maturity are inseparable. It is impossible to be spiritually mature while remaining emotionally immature."
> - Peter Scazzero.

Prepare for Discipline as they Grow.

Parenting evolves as children grow, but many parents underestimate how drastically their role changes. For some, parenting seems to center around providing groceries, healthcare, and clean home without anticipating the challenges of discipline that inevitably come with age.

The truth is, no child matures without discipline. Even God, in His infinite love, chastises us as His children. A good harvest requires timely pruning. While women are incredibly resilient and nurturing, instilling discipline can be challenging, and having support makes a difference.

I have observed countless situations where children misbehave in front of their mothers but instantly straighten up when their fathers appear. The mere presence of a father often commands a level of respect and obedience that mothers alone might struggle to achieve.

I know children who shout at their moms and misbehave yet remain silent when their dads step in. Unfortunately, that was not my experience.

A Mother's Voice as the Sole Authority

My mom was the sole authority in my teenage years, alongside my teachers at school. At school, I avoided trouble because I did not want to face punishment. At home, my mom's tough-love approach kept me in check. She did not punish me often, but when she did, it was serious enough to leave a lasting impression. I learned quickly to avoid trouble, even when it felt nearly impossible.

Things began to change as I grew older. One incident stands out vividly in my memory. I was suspended at 18 for something I hadn't considered serious then, but it was the worst mistake I'd made in my six years of high school. During every academic assembly, it was customary for the best students to shake hands with their teachers after being announced by their class teachers. I was the only one in my class who qualified on this occasion. Having done it many times before, I didn't think much of it and chose not to stand up. This seemingly small act upset the entire staff, who had never seen me display such perceived indiscipline.

It was a moment that marked a significant turning point, as their disappointment weighed heavily on me. I expected my mom to punish me severely, but to my surprise, she did not. Instead, she took me to school and asked for pardon on my behalf. Another time, during my vacation, she encouraged me to pursue my passion for tailoring. She arranged for me to live with my uncle and attend his tailoring institute, which I gladly did.

Yet, as university time approached, I overheard her discussing a more affordable technical school option where I could focus on tailoring, hoping I might attend university later. Though I was truly passionate about fashion, I couldn't imagine not going to university like the rest of the students in my former class. I did not agree but chose not to argue. Instead, I took a taxi home, secured my university admission, and presented it to her. She was not pleased, but there was not much she could do, and physical punishment was no longer an option.

Breaking the Rules and Finding Freedom

Once I joined the university, my independence began to grow. If my mom disagreed with me, I acted on my own. For instance, my school ministry often organized church missions, and when she refused to let me go, I went anyway without permission. After one semester, I told her I'd visit my paternal grandmother, but instead, I caught a 2:00 a.m. bus with a friend for a mission trip to the Kyenjojo district.

When she realized and called the first day, I did not pick up. By the second day, I answered, and she told me to come home immediately. Once back, she asked me to write an apology letter. I complied without hesitation, penning a formal "Dear Madam..." introduction as we had been taught in business communication class that semester. Instead of diffusing the situation, my formality infuriated her further. She was furious, but I was not fazed because I wrote it intentionally. I knew she could not spank me anymore.

This pattern repeated itself. While she thought I was at my friend's hostel studying for exams the following year, I left for another mission trip to Iganga. After two days of unanswered calls, a friend persuaded me to answer by asking, "Do you know the pain of childbirth?" That worked! I finally picked up, told my mom where I was, and promised to return soon.

You might think I was a rebellious child, and maybe I was. But at least I was rebelling by going to the right places, and by God's grace, I was protected. However, think about children who escape to questionable places because they do not respect their parents' rules.

Reflecting on my experiences, I believe having another voice of authority in my life might have prevented some of my defiance. I was used to my mom's rules and eager to push against the limits whenever possible because I knew she could no longer punish me.

Authority and Respect

As an adult, I have realized this pattern has affected many areas of my life. As I have already shared, I hated it whenever our mom exercised authority over us. I felt she was being unfair and dominant and couldn't wait to escape it. The only authority I have never questioned is that of my pastors. However, in other relationships, I need explanations, not commands. Authority needs to be delivered with love, respect, and understanding. Without these, I instinctively resist or seek a way out.

One incident stands out vividly. My friends and I were planning a trip to New York. When I mentioned it to my boyfriend, he said he could not join because of work. That was fine with me, and I was going regardless. Later, one of my friends revealed that her boyfriend did not allow her to go. I was shocked and exclaimed, "What? Is he your dad?" My reaction became a running joke among my friends.

It is not that I dislike authority; I value it when it is rooted in mutual respect. But commands without explanations trigger resistance in me. I have carried this lesson from childhood, shaped by my interactions with my mom and the absence of a second parental voice to balance the discipline and understanding I needed.

The Need for Balanced Parenting

Parenting requires more than provision; it requires balanced discipline, emotional support, and the presence of both authority and understanding. My mom did her best as a single parent, but looking back, I realize how the absence of a father's voice shaped my responses to authority.

Every child needs guidance, and ideally, that guidance comes from parents working together to provide balance. Without this, children often test boundaries and push limits in ways that might be avoided with additional support. As adults, we carry these patterns into our relationships, workplaces, and interactions, often struggling to balance respect and independence.

The key is learning to approach authority with love and understanding, whether as a parent, mentor, or partner. Children, need discipline and structure but also explanations, respect, and room to grow. When authority is balanced with empathy, it creates a foundation for lasting respect and mutual trust.

Babysitting

My mom shared a story from when I was very young, likely before I was sent to live in the village. At the time, she worked as a nursery teacher and had to rely on babysitters while she was at work. I was a fussy, crying baby, and my babysitter often became so overwhelmed that she would leave me outside under the sun. My mom believes this is why my skin is darker than she expected. hahaha. It is a story she still mentions today.

While I do not remember those early experiences vividly, I know they impacted me. Babysitters, after all, often shape the behaviors and attitudes of the children they care for, especially during formative years.

Having been both a babysitter and someone who was babysat, I can confidently say that the person you entrust with your child matters greatly. Babysitters often significantly influence children, sometimes even more than the parents. I remember babysitting for a family whose children quickly began imitating me. Within a week, they sang the songs I listened to, watched the shows I enjoyed, and mimicked my behaviors. Thankfully, this was a Christian household, so the influence was positive. I prayed with them, watched sermons, and prepared their meals. But this experience opened my eyes to how easily children absorb what they see and hear, even in a short period.

The Risks of Choosing the Babysitter

Imagine leaving your children with someone who does not share your values. What if your child's first words were curse words they heard from a babysitter? Or worse, what if they were exposed to behaviors or ideologies that distort their sense of identity? While bad things can happen anywhere, some influences are entirely avoidable.

I once visited a home where a woman was babysitting several children. One baby needed a diaper change, and the babysitter, clearly irritated, began yelling at the child. My heart broke as I watched her dismiss the baby's cries. I was not someone who naturally adored babies. As a young girl, people usually asked my sister for babysitting help, not me, but I knew that yelling at a baby was unacceptable.

Even though I did not change my first diaper until I was 24, I would never let a child suffer because of it. Moments like that emphasize the importance of choosing caregivers who treat your child with love and respect.

Babysitting is a sensitive topic, especially for working parents who rely on others to care for their children. But we must be vigilant. Please pay attention to the environments where you leave your kids and listen closely when they try to share their experiences. Children's confidence and self-esteem are often shaped or shattered by those entrusted with their care. If you notice sudden behavioral changes in your child, it is worth considering whether they've picked up negative influences from their babysitters.

The Role of Parents in a Babysitter-Dependent World

As parents, we can't control everything, but we shouldn't delegate our parenting responsibility to others. Babysitters play an important role, but the foundational lessons, such as affirming a child's identity and speaking life into them, are our responsibility. The world is increasingly chaotic, and many harmful influences come from people close to our children. The devil often uses these avenues to plant deception and confusion about who they are.

Unfortunately, some children have even been harmed by relatives who were supposed to be trusted caregivers. This underscores the importance of being intentional about who you allow into your child's life. Babysitters who share your values and love your children deserve recognition. Celebrate and appreciate those genuinely caring for your kids; their role is invaluable. Babysitting is not an easy job, and those who do it well deserve more than minimum wage; they deserve respect and gratitude.

The Value of Appreciation

I have encountered people who denied their babysitters fair pay, an injustice I can't overlook.

Babysitters shoulder a tremendous responsibility, and no amount of money can truly compensate for their care. However, what they deserve, at the very least, is respect and appreciation. If someone is looking after your children, especially if they're doing it well, they contribute to your family in ways that can never be repaid.

In today's work-driven culture, babysitters are essential. Some parents even find it a relief to be away from their kids for a while, which only highlights how much patience and effort babysitters put into their work. The least we can do is show them love and appreciation. At the same time, we need to ensure we are spending meaningful time with our children. Parents sometimes know little about their kids because babysitters handle so much of their care.

Be cautious about who you entrust with your children. Choose babysitters who fear God and share your values, as their influence is profound. If you're fortunate to find someone who genuinely loves and cares for your kids, show them appreciation in words and actions.

I hope to see more Christians rise to create childcare and daycare programs grounded in the fear of God. Our children deserve to be raised in environments that nurture their hearts and minds, shaping them into the people God created them to be. Let us avoid entrusting our children to those not sharing these values, ensuring they grow up in a safe, loving, and affirming environment.

Mothers and ladies have always carried incredible strength and resilience, often standing in the gap for absent fathers. Their sacrifices and unwavering dedication have shaped many lives, including my own. Yet, even in their efforts comes a sobering truth: time is irreplaceable. It is not just what we provide for our children, but the presence we give that leaves the deepest impact. Deliberating with our time shapes relationships, builds trust, and leaves lasting legacies in our children.

As single mothers, we need community.
you can't do this alone."
-Evelin Viera, at Photizo Daily

CHAPTER TWELVE

BE DELIBERATE—MAKE TIME

"Fatherhood is not just a position but a mission. God has entrusted children to us to lead, love, and nurture toward Him."
– David Platt.

When we moved in with my mom, she took a no-nonsense approach to parenting. She made us handle everything ourselves: chores, responsibilities, and problem-solving. We hated it. No matter how overwhelmed we felt, she would not help. It was sinking or swimming. My sister, unable to handle the constant clashes with my mom, after some years, eventually left to live with one of our grandmothers. Their arguments were relentless, and one day, I came home to find my sister gone. My mom did not offer much explanation, only saying she had moved out.

With my sister gone, the full weight of housework fell on me. I thought the workload would make me sick, hahaha, but surprisingly, it did not. Instead, it taught me resilience. I learned how to manage a home, multitask, and handle responsibilities without expecting someone else to bail me out. Those tough years built the foundation for the work ethic and independence I carry today.

Over time, my mom began to trust me more. She started leaving me in charge of the shop, house, and even our cousins during holidays. Many people admire my ability to juggle multiple tasks, but few know where it all began. Those lessons in self-reliance were forged through necessity under my mom's tough love. Although she spent much of our early years traveling for work, she made a point to focus on teaching us life skills during our high school years. It was not that our grandmother hadn't taught us anything; she had. But my mom saw gaps in our knowledge that she felt compelled to fill, and she worked hard to ensure we would be prepared for life.

Parenting through Changing Lenses

Parenting styles evolve and seeing how parents treat their grandchildren differently from their children is fascinating. My mom, for instance, often seemed surprised that we did not learn certain things growing up, yet she was not there to teach us during our formative years. To this day, this can lead to disagreements.

Why do some parents expect kids to have manners they didn't instill? They have their kids misbehaving all the time before them, and when they go out with them, they want them to behave otherwise and even pretend they are seeing such behavior for the first time. Didn't we learn that charity begins at home? I know children can act up and be embarrassing sometimes, but if you teach them early, you save yourself so much embarrassment when they grow.

I resented always being compared to other kids. My mom would hold us to the same standards as children whose parents had been actively involved in their lives. But how could we be expected to measure up when we had an unconventional upbringing?

In Luganda, a proverb says, ***"Once something is bent, when you try to straighten it, it just breaks."*** That saying resonates deeply because so much of what we become is shaped early in life as we grow. The first seven years of a child's life are so critical. It is important to know what they see, hear, and do.

Our mom worked hard to provide for us, just as many parents do today, but time spent working often meant less time bonding, teaching, or guiding. Thankfully, she made an intentional effort later to instill valuable lessons in us, redeeming what she could.

The Modern Parenting Dilemma

Today, many parents, especially single parents, are consumed by work. While providing for children's physical needs is essential, parenting requires more than putting food on the table. Children also need love, guidance, and discipline. Too often, we rely on babysitters, teachers, or older siblings to fill the gaps, neglecting the deeper responsibility of raising well-rounded individuals.

It is heartbreaking to find teenagers who do not even know how to make their beds or clean up after themselves because they were never taught. Teaching children responsibility isn't just about lightening the household workload but preparing them for life. You're equipping them with skills that will serve them well into adulthood by giving them chores and holding them accountable. Though I hated it as a teenager when my mom gave me all the housework, today, I am thankful she did. Life is more serious than the present fear I see some parents have, the fear of hurting their feelings.

Investing in Your Children

Raising children is one of the most important investments we'll ever make. As parents, we need to go beyond the basics. We must intentionally shape their character, teach them discipline, and prepare them to navigate the world confidently and competently.

- Teach them life skills: Whether cooking, cleaning, or managing money, equip your children with practical knowledge so they can thrive independently.
- Lead with love and intention: Balance discipline with kindness. Listen to your children, guide them patiently, and let them know they're valued.
- Foster independence: Encourage them to take ownership of their responsibilities, helping them build confidence and resilience.

Remember, you're not raising children to hand off to someone else; you are raising future leaders. Be intentional, start early, show them love, and prepare them to be disciplined, capable, and responsible men and women God has made them. Your efforts today will shape who they become tomorrow.

Being deliberate with our time is the foundation of meaningful connections. However, the quality of that time depends on the strength of the relationships we build within our families. Family and romantic relationships are not always easy; they require patience, understanding, and grace. Chapter thirteen explores the complex dynamics of family and relationships and how they shape our identities, challenge our growth, and provide opportunities for healing and reconciliation.

> *"I do not know how my kids always know when I'm almost home, but every time I walk in, they're at the door, ready to hug me, shouting, 'Daddy's home!'*
> *At that moment, all the day's stress disappears."*
> *- Eddie K. S at Photizo Daily.*

CHAPTER THIRTEEN

FAMILY AND RELATIONSHIPS

How you represent God in your home will shape how your children view Him. Will they confidently call upon the God of their father, as we see among the patriarchs in scripture?

The Day I Cried Out to My Mum

By now, you probably understand that I did not have a close relationship with my family growing up. My mother was more of a provider than an emotional support system, someone I called when I needed something: tuition, supplies, transport, or medical help.

Beyond that, there was not much attachment. She fulfilled her responsibilities, but her financial discipline often frustrated me. For instance, she would send just enough for tuition and not a shilling more, and that never sat well with me. I used to dream of the day when I would not have to depend on her for anything.

As I grew older, I prided myself on becoming self-sufficient. Vulnerability was not an option, especially with my mother, because I had not learned it. While I freely shared with friends and mentors, I kept my pain hidden from her. This lack of connection shaped me into someone who poured my energy into books, soccer, and music, keeping relationships at a distance, particularly with my family.

ENDLESS QUEST

Friendships over Family

Friendships became my anchor. My life revolved around them, especially as my faith deepened and I became active in church. I opened my heart to many friends, making them my chosen family, as my bond with my biological family remained tenuous.

During college, I remember how disconnected I was at home. I'd come in, grab food in one hand, my phone in the other, and retreat to my world. My mother, after days of observation, finally confronted me:

"Do you think you live in a forest? You have no conversation with the people in this house! You come, eat, sleep, and leave early in the morning!"

I brushed her off. I was glued to my phone, sending hundreds of texts daily. It did not bother me that I had no meaningful interactions with my family; my attention was elsewhere.

At one point, my mother also criticized my giving habits. I was generous, but only toward my friends and church community, not my family. She called me out: "So, you'd rather spend your money and time on strangers than your sister or cousins?"

It stung, but I justified it to myself, thinking they did not make me happy like my church friends. Looking back, I see how misguided that thinking was.

A Wake-Up Call

The turning point came in 2019 when my world seemed to crumble after a painful breakup. What I thought was the worst heartbreak imaginable turned into an even bigger storm. On September 24, my OGs and friends started sending me screenshots of a Ugandan blogger's post accusing me of destroying people's marriages. Attached to the post were my photo and a baseless claim that I was behaving contrary to my faith.

I was devastated. Betrayed by people I had loved, and thought were friends, I felt the entire world was against me. For the first time, I called my mother for help: emotional support. I texted her, "Maama, please pray for me." It was a moment of vulnerability I had never allowed myself to show her. I was exhausted emotionally, spiritually, and mentally. Yet, even as I thought everything was falling apart, God was not done with me. He carried me through that storm, leaving me with a valuable lesson: You need your family.

The Importance of Investing in Family

That experience pushed me back toward the same family I had neglected. I realized that family bonds are irreplaceable and worth nurturing. I learned to rebuild those relationships diligently, pray for my family, prioritize them, and speak well of them.

For years, I wished I had been born into a different family, but wishing changed nothing. Love and prayers, however, did. I understood that God placed me in this family for a reason, even if I did not initially see it. Some of us take our families for granted, but I have learned to cherish mine. My relationship with my mother and sister has grown tremendously.

Friendships and Relationships as Young Adult

As I navigated friendships and relationships, I often found myself confused by people's intentions. I tended to interpret everyone's kindness as purely platonic, whether they were my peers or older mentors. This naivety sometimes led to misunderstandings, where people expected more from me than I realized.

For example, when I had just joined college, a man gave me a smartphone as a gift. I was thrilled, especially since the phone my mom had bought me wasn't a smart one. Little did I know, his gift came with strings attached, and he sought a romantic relationship. When I didn't reciprocate his feelings, he asked for the phone back, hahaha. A few months later, another older acquaintance suddenly showed interest in me, saying he wanted to marry me after I graduated.

At 19, marriage was the last thing on my mind. I told him I valued his company and wanted to remain friends, but he bluntly replied that he wasn't looking for friendship with a 19-year-old, which was the end of him, hahaha. These experiences opened my eyes to the reality that not everyone's actions are as straightforward as they seem.

I also struggled with understanding my own emotions. I often sought validation from people who did not value me as much as I valued them, leading to unnecessary conflicts and heartbreak. But through it all, God preserved me. I am grateful for the parents who raised respectful, God-fearing men who did not exploit my naivety.

Breaking Cycles and Moving Forward

Reflecting on these experiences, I realized how much I did not know about romantic or otherwise relationships. I have needlessly been hurt and even hurt some people unintentionally. I wish I had known then what I know now. Many conflicts could have been avoided if I had been more self-aware and intentional in my interactions.

Parents play a crucial role in preparing their children for relationships, especially with the opposite sex. Without proper guidance, children are likely to repeat cycles of misunderstanding and pain. Teaching children how to navigate relationships with wisdom and respect can save them and future generations from unnecessary heartache.

Despite my missteps, I thank God for His protection and grace. He has preserved me through challenges and used them to shape me into a better, more self-aware person. Today, I am committed to building healthier relationships with my family and others and seeking God's guidance at every step of my journey.

God has saved me from many traps! There is a saying in my language that I learned as an adult, and we often made fun of it with my friends about guys who literally would kill anyone just to have your attention. The saying, **"Teli alumilirwa nga talina kigendelerwa,"** literally translates to "nobody cares or is so concerned about you without a hidden agenda."

Though, as Christians, we have learned of God's command to love, serve, and help those in need, after seven years in Boston, I can somewhat agree with that proverb, yes, even in church! I could write a book that agrees with it, even among believers.

I appreciate so many people who have helped me and will say it is true there are genuinely kind people. However, I cannot miss saying that some men will run to help you when you think they are so kind, yet all they want is a piece of you. *"What? I thought you were being a nice brother"* I always wondered. hahaha. But what happened to simply being humane? Okay, what about just being followers of Christ, who says, "Whatsoever you do to the least of the brothers, you do it unto me"?

In this generation, where young Christian women to look up to are scarce, God blessed me with Mama Vivienne. I was raised Catholic, so I did not have an idea about how to go about this Salvation life! Mama Vivienne quickly stepped in. From the numerous 'silly' questions I had to the different experiences, the bad and ugly, her inbox has always been open to me! She has availed herself to listen to me and not judge me, encourage me, and pray with me, which is rare these days.

She may not know this, but her presence in my life has played a huge role in the kind of Christian I am today. She's one of those very few people who believe in the call of God upon my life, one that I must say isn't so clear to me yet! Sometimes, I wonder what she sees in me but trust me when I say we all need such people. Mama Vivienne is a lover of men who teaches you without even trying hard, a humble, simple, but very deep woman of God. God knew I needed such a gem, and I could not be more grateful! I love you, Mama, and thank God for bringing you into my life."

~ Sylvia

Reflections from My Dysfunctional Romantic Relationships

Emotional Abuse and Narcissism in Relationships

Before I learned about emotional abuse, I had only heard the word "abuse" concerning child abuse. Seven years ago, when I had just moved here, someone used the term in a completely new way. An ex-partner of someone I knew casually mentioned that her ex was an abusive man. "Really?" I thought to myself. "But he's so kind and good to me. What do you mean he's abusive?"

I did not dwell on it until I witnessed a friend in a relationship that raised countless red flags. The man she was with was dishonest, disrespectful, and lacked character. Yet, despite his obvious flaws, she stayed. She was confused by the occasional moments that looked like love, forgetting the abuse she was enduring. She was always running after him, even though he was a compulsive liar. I did not use the word "abusive" at the time, but I began to understand what that other woman meant. It became even clearer when I entered my relationships.

My Quest for a Love So Pure!

All my life, I had looked forward to a relationship where we would be in love, agreeable, happy, and do many things together. But sadly, that was not my experience. Have you ever known someone who says they love you, but 98% of their actions say otherwise? I questioned everything I thought I knew about love.

- *Did I learn wrong when they said love brings out the best in you?*
- *Did I dream wrong that a romantic relationship or marriage is supposed to be our safe place?*
- *Did I do wrong to give my time to someone who wrote endless love messages but stopped as soon as they had me? I started to wonder if I was the problem.*
- *Was I demanding too much by speaking up about wanting flowers, occasional outings, or love shown in my love language instead of what my partner rigidly offered?*
- *Did I do wrong to ask about his upbringing and family, or why did he never mention me in his plans?*

I remember asking one man what he thought about me getting orthodontic treatment for my teeth. His response was, "I love you the way you are. You're already cute and fine."

But I did not love myself the way I was. I had been insecure about my teeth for over 15 years. I went ahead with the treatment, and four months later, that relationship ended. Hahaha. This may seem trivial, but it was not to me; it was dismissal. It reflected a much larger issue: an inability to feel supported and valued in the relationship.

I know many people who have staked their destinies and lives in relationships where they are unseen, unvalued, and excluded. I, too, once found myself in a similar situation.

There was a time when I was in a relationship where we seemed to be doing everything together, sharing time, experiences, and dreams. But one day, I realized he never mentioned my name in everything he built. Not even in passing. It stung even more because I was not dependent on him. My independence had enabled him to save and achieve so much in a short time. And yet, I was absent from his plans.

I finally mustered the courage to ask him directly, "Why don't you ever include me in what you're building?"

His response left me speechless: *"When I use 'me' or 'I,' I mean 'we.'"*

What? How does that even work? How does using "me" or "I" include "us" when it is clear I'm not part of the equation? Hahaha. That moment opened my eyes. While I poured my time, effort, and emotions into this relationship, he was building a future that did not include me. it was not about love or the relationship we were building, it was about convenience.

Ladies, you do not have to agree with me, but I want my child to read this one day. Avoid people who shy away from speaking about their plans and true feelings concerning you. Run from anyone who refuses to open up about their background. These are the things that build understanding and connection in a relationship. If someone can't share their past or define their reason for being with you, how can you build a future with them? I have suffered these things in the past!

Accountability matters. If someone refuses to be accountable to you, their words, or the relationship, you'll find yourself navigating a maze of confusion, distrust, and pain. And let me say this clearly: run; do not walk from anyone who wants to keep you a secret. There is no honor in secrecy when it comes to love. If someone loves you, they want to celebrate, include, and proudly acknowledge you.

A relationship built on avoidance, secrecy, and lack of accountability is no relationship at all; it is a trap. I have suffered most of these traps! So, choose wisely, and do not settle for less than someone who can love you openly, honestly, and fully.

Toxicity Rooted in Our Past

I know many of us like I used to, struggle to identify toxic relationships because they mirror where we come from. No one told us we were loved and valued, and no one ever told us we were beautiful. For some of us, people never kept their promises, and love was never spelt out in bold.

So, when someone calls us "cute," it feels like a breakthrough, even if their words do not align with their actions. We accept mistreatment because we do not know what healthy love looks like.

Perhaps some of us are toxic because we, too, have been abused or even because that's all we've learned from childhood. I find it important for us to know how to recognize narcissism right away because it is why many of us are suffering drama in relationships, marriage or even co-parenting. We did not recognize this earlier!

Recognizing Emotional Abuse and Narcissism

Emotional abuse is a pattern of behavior used to manipulate, control, and degrade someone, leaving invisible scars. It targets a person's sense of self-worth and security.

Signs of Emotional Abuse:

1. Constant criticism: Pointing out flaws and making you feel inadequate.
2. Gas lighting: Making you doubt your perceptions or memory.
3. Silent treatment: Withdrawing communication to punish or control.
4. Control: Monitoring your activities, forcing you into things you don't want, isolating you, or controlling finances.
5. Blame-shifting: Never take accountability and make you feel responsible.
6. Emotional manipulation Using guilt, fear, or affection as tools to control.

Effects of Emotional Abuse:

- Loss of self-esteem.
- Chronic anxiety or depression.
- Difficulty trusting others or forming healthy relationships.

Narcissism in Relationships

Narcissism involves an inflated sense of self-importance, a need for admiration, and a lack of empathy.

In relationships, it manifests as manipulation, control, and exploitation.

Signs of Narcissistic Behavior:

1. Lack of empathy Dismissing your emotions or needs.
2. Love-bombing: Excessive charm at first, followed by devaluation.
3. Self-centeredness: Making everything about them.
4. Manipulation: Using your vulnerabilities against you.
5. Exploitation: Taking advantage of your kindness or resources.

Effects of Narcissistic Relationships:

- Emotional exhaustion from meeting their demands.
- Confusion and self-doubt caused by gas lighting.
- Isolation from loved ones.

Final Thoughts:

Just because someone seems kind in public does not mean they're the same in private.

Abuse, whether emotional or physical, is abuse. Period. We need to stop victimizing people who speak up about it. Understanding the signs of emotional abuse and narcissism can empower us to make better choices and support those in need.

Celebrating Love and Acknowledging Pain

First, I want to celebrate and honor everyone married, especially those who have found joy and purpose in their union. You inspire me, and I hope to join your ranks soon; please keep me in your prayers. My heart goes out to those enduring the pain of breakups, separations, or divorces. I have walked that road, and while no one prepared me for the pain of those experiences, I have learned how deeply we need kindness and understanding during such times.

Breakups are often a whirlwind of emotions, hurt, betrayal, and loss, followed by the challenge of rebuilding your life without the person, places, and routines you once shared. It is not a clean break; it is a storm you weather, piece by piece.

The Decision to Break Away

Please do not mistake that for ease when I say I walked away from certain relationships. Every decision to leave was heavy with doubt, grief, and second-guessing.

While some celebrate breakups and divorces as newfound freedom, it is an emotionally grueling process for many of us. Still, I have learned that leaving a dysfunctional relationship today is far better than staying trapped in a broken future. Some fatherless homes today are because they ignored breaking away before getting married, yet the signs were obvious; some married for the wrong reasons, had children, and now suffer consequences.

I refused to settle for a life of disrespect, toxicity, or emotional neglect. I wanted a future of love, honor, and peace, a life where I was cherished and not tolerated. It takes courage to leave unhealthy spaces, but the journey toward healing is worth it.

Hard Lessons about Love and Relationships

Through my experiences, I have learned that not everyone who claims to love you truly does. Being in the church or growing older does not necessarily equate to maturity or alignment with Christ-like character. I have also learned not to lean on my understanding. My mistakes resulted from rushing ahead without waiting for God's guidance or ignoring His voice.

Though I eagerly wanted to be married in my first relationship, I now realize I was driven more by the desire for a wedding and societal pressure than by a genuine connection that truly matters to me. I was not mentally or emotionally prepared for marriage. I was young and naive, and my character needed refinement before I could seriously discuss such a commitment. Marriage requires a depth of maturity and readiness that I did not possess.

Although I constantly talked about marriage, I can honestly say I was more fascinated by the idea of a wedding than the reality of marriage itself, a reality whose vision and model I did not yet understand. Looking back, I see now that I could never have thrived with someone who could not lead and protect me.

Yet, I did not even consider that at the start of the relationship. I entered the relationship out of pity, and eventually, when I grew tired of playing the role of a "mother" and no longer felt pitiful, I found myself endlessly asking, "What am I doing here?" Hahaha. There was no connection, genuine love, humor, or defined purpose!

Marriage should be founded on sober judgment, love, friendship, God, a clear vision, and purpose, but no one had taught me this. Some might say, "But you were old enough!" or "You were in church!" Parents, it is not the pastor's responsibility to nurture your children. From experience and study, I have learned that submitting to someone who cannot lead, provide, or protect is nearly impossible.

Healing and Growth

My second relationship taught me the importance of boundaries, self-love, and knowing what I want. I lost myself in that relationship, clinging to the hope that things would change. But toxic people rarely change for as long as you stay; they often make you more like them.

I did not know where I stood emotionally for a long time. All I knew was that I wanted to get married. But how crazy is it to plan a future with someone who does not want you, does not include you in their plans, and is emotionally unavailable?

I watched Steve Harvey's talk show, particularly the "Ask Uncle Steve" segment, during that season. One episode stuck with me: a woman asked how to make her partner, who had been abusive and stayed with her for 13 years without engagement or marriage, commit to her. Uncle Steve's response was blunt and powerful: *"Do you want another 13 years of the same experience?"* That question hit me hard.

His show became instrumental in helping me understand my worth and building the strength I needed to break free. I'm thankful for Uncle Steve and his shows, which educate women about men and relationships. What has amazed me over time is that women of all ages will be troubled and asking what you would think is basic about men. hahaha. He has taught me so much, especially how men think and what they mean when they do and say certain things.

Though some people troll him for giving relationship and marriage advice, I admire his humor, love, and commitment to sharing what he's learned and using his experiences to help others. Though I only watch him on social media and TV, He is a father figure. Because of his show's impact on me during a dark and hopeless season, I'd love to meet him one day and thank him in person. He's helped countless people, and I'm one of them. I hope more grown men can arise in our communities and speak up!

One piece of advice that took me a long time to accept fully was this: **"Never let a man tell you twice that he does not want you."** That truth hit hard as someone who lived in denial and stayed in the wrong places for too long. Uncle Steve pushed some much-needed common sense into my head. I have learned that men know exactly what they want, and they communicate it, though it may take a while for our emotions to catch up. Men know who they want to be with, and in my experience, even if they do not want you, some will keep you around for the benefits you bring, even when they do not see a future with you.

You're wasting your time with someone whose heart shifted 2,899 years ago. Like that woman who spent 13 years in a toxic relationship, I did the same, thinking endurance was a sign of love. But true love does not leave you bitter, drained, or questioning your worth. It should inspire you, bring out your best, and make you feel valued daily.

The Power of Sisterhood

During my hardest times, I found solace in the company of two female friends. Their support reminded me of the strength that comes from a sisterhood rooted in love and understanding. The devil often attacks female friendships, sowing division through jealousy, betrayal, or romantic entanglements.

I have learned to protect these bonds. A man who disrespects your friend or pursues multiple women within the same circle isn't worth anyone's time. We must refuse to let men fracture the relationships we've built with other women. Be your sister's keeper and hold onto those tried-and-true friendships.

Taking Breaks and Seeking God

One mistake many of us make is rushing into a new relationship before we've healed from the last. We jump from person to person, accumulating emotional baggage and losing ourselves. Instead, we need to take intentional breaks to seek God, care for ourselves, and surround ourselves with people who love us unconditionally.

The story of the Samaritan woman at the well with Jesus reminds me that transformation is possible when we encounter Christ. Healing takes time, but it is worth it.

Rediscovering Self-Worth

Breaking away from toxic relationships meant facing financial and emotional challenges, but it also meant rediscovering my worth. I deserve respect, love, and honor. Through prayer, self-reflection, and personal growth, I have become stronger.

This process has not only prepared me for future relationships but also deepened my relationships with

God, my family, and myself. Take the time to know who you are; you're worth it. You deserve a love that builds you up, not tears you down. Take breaks to heal.

Do not jump into relationships out of fear or loneliness. Cherish your friendships. They can be a source of strength during your hardest times. Trust God's timing. He knows what you need and when you need it.

My Little Sisters and dear younger ones

I write with love and a desire to see you live a life that reflects your God-given worth and purpose. I see some of you often and can't help but wish I had known what I know now when I was your age. While I can't change my past, I can share these lessons with you, hoping they help you make wiser choices than I did.

Listen to Your Spirit

Deep down, we always sense whether something is good or bad for us. When something is right, it brings peace; when it is wrong, there is always a sense of unease. The problem is that we often silence that inner voice, deceiving ourselves because we are caught up in our emotions.

I know this because I have done it. Every wrong relationship I have been involved in had signs that I knew in my spirit was not right, but I ignored those warnings. I let my feelings take over, neglecting what my spirit and mind told me. It cost me dearly.

That's why I'm urging you to listen to the voice of your spirit. Pay attention to what God is showing you, even if it does not align with your feelings.

Trust God, Not Your Feelings

The Bible says: *"Trust in the Lord with all your heart and lean not on your own understanding" (Proverbs 3:5, NIV).* Feelings can be good but fleeting and often deceptive, yet God's guidance is always true and reliable. If you trust God and surrender your choices, He will lead you into His perfect plan. Do not let anyone pressure you into something unhealthy or dishonorable to Him. Nothing is worth compromising your peace, values, or relationship with Him. If it does not honor God, you are better off without it.

Know Your Worth

You are not defined by what others think of you; you do not need a relationship to validate your identity. Your worth comes from God, who loves you unconditionally. Jesus died for you, and that makes you priceless.

You do not need to look outside yourself for fulfillment. True satisfaction comes from knowing who you are in Christ and trusting Him to meet your needs. Learn to love yourself as He loves you; never let the world convince you otherwise.

Work on What Matters

This is the time to focus on the things that truly matter. Work on your dreams, discover your purpose, and pursue what God has placed in your heart. Do not let fear or impatience make you settle for less than you deserve.

You have so much potential, and your dreams are valid. Use this season to grow, build, and prepare for what God has in store for you.

Be Teachable and Accountable

It is easy to think you have it all figured out when you're young. But wisdom often comes from experience, and those who've walked the road you're on can see things you may not. Do not despise good counsel!

I remember my mentee dating someone I knew was not right for her. I warned her, "If you go down this path, you'll cry yourself to sleep." I spoke from experience because I had been through the same. She seemed to understand, but not long after, she ignored the warning and did exactly what I cautioned against. She cried, just as I had told her she would.

When someone who cares about you speaks from experience, it is not to control you but to protect you from pain. Be humble enough to listen and teachable to learn, especially if you trust the person speaking to you.

Do not Settle for Less.

You are worth far more than the world will ever acknowledge. Do not hesitate to walk away if someone does not see your value or treat you with respect and love. Being single is not a curse, as society pushes us to think most of the time; it is a season of growth and preparation for something better.

One man once said, "You would rather be single than taken for granted." Some people may seem to be in relationships, but what they truly are is taken for granted. As someone who once compromised my values for others, I can tell you without hesitation that it's not worth it.

You Are Enough

Like I was, some of us find ourselves in places where we are often made to feel inadequate. But here's the truth: You are beautiful, strong, and deeply loved by God.

The Bible says: "For I know the plans I have for you," declares the Lord, "plans to prosper you and not to harm you, plans to give you hope and a future" (Jeremiah 29:11, NIV).

Though I do not have it all together, I have learned that your worth is non-negotiable. Listen to your spirit, trust in God, stay true to your values, and pursue the things that matter most. Above all, remember that you are loved beyond measure by the One who made you. Amen.

Transitions

A transition is a shift from one state or situation to another, encompassing personal, emotional, or social changes. Transitions can be planned or unplanned, but they always require adaptation. This process often evokes uncertainty, fear, or anxiety as the outcomes remain unknown.

Transitions test our ability to adapt, whether starting a new job, moving, or facing significant life events. However, they also offer an opportunity to grow. Embracing transitions means recognizing their significance and finding ways to navigate the accompanying challenges with resilience.

Struggling with Change

Like many of us, I have often struggled with embracing transitions, unsure whether the difficulties I faced were lessons meant to strengthen me or the result of being unprepared. Life has taught me that change is inevitable, but preparation can make it less jarring.

While I value learning through experience, I understand the importance of equipping oneself mentally and emotionally for change. Preparation is a principle I deeply value, even knowing that life often surprises us despite our plans.

Growing up, I was surrounded by consistency. My mom and grandma were steadfast in their actions, people of integrity. Whatever they said, they did. Whatever they had to do, they did promptly. My mom never failed to visit us on Sundays, and my grandma ensured meals were on the table at set times every day. Their reliability shaped me into a person who values structure and dislikes excuses.

I am the kind that gets things done. Though this is beautiful, it also made me clash when I met people who are far different. When I encountered people or situations that did not align with this level of dependability, like my father's inconsistency, I could not cope. Instead of learning that the world does not revolve around me, I cut him off. I am still learning this.

My upbringing left me unprepared for life's inevitable shifts. While I applaud my mom and grandma for being incredible role models as people of integrity, which is so important to me, I have also had to learn that life comes with shocks, detours, liars, haters, and all sorts of people. I have learned that life is not linear, so I have had to slow down, be patient with myself, and embrace change, even when it feels overwhelming.

Embracing Self-Acceptance Amidst Change

As a child, I struggled with self-esteem, comparing my short stature and dark skin to my taller, lighter-skinned sister. Society reinforced the belief that light skin equals beauty until I attended an all-girls high school. Initially, I did not know the school was same sex; it was a shock. I remember my grandma taking me there, and I kept looking around, but I couldn't see any boys in the school.

So, during night preps, I saw some students walk in dressed in shorts, and I thought maybe we just had a few boys. In the morning, the very kids I saw in shorts were in skirts. I was shocked and then gradually processed the reality. I embraced my uniqueness by observing the students' carefree attitudes and confidence in their individuality there.

Over time, I learned to appreciate my body and found confidence outside societal norms.

Transitions in Relationships

Change became even more challenging when it involved relationships. My first breakup was a harsh wake-up call. Walking into spaces where I had once shared memories with someone became unbearable.

The pain of separation lingered, even though I initiated the breakup. I could not eat or cook for a month, and my mom, noticing my weight loss, innocently asked if my relationship was not making me happy. She had no idea it had ended months before.

Although God had given me multiple warnings about these relationships, I ignored them because I was desperate to get married. When the breakups came, I realized how unprepared I was for the emotional fallout. God is always speaking, and it is up to us to listen and hearken.

Another sign of a significant transition came during a trip with my then-boyfriend and friends. What should have been a joyful experience turned painful as my boyfriend openly flirted with a friend in my presence.

So, I decided to walk fast and leave them, and that two-mile trek in silence became a moment of hearing God; I sensed a shift in my life approaching, and I could feel deep within my spirit that a move was coming. Yet, instead of seeking God for clarity and guidance, my attention was consumed by the actions of my narcissistic boyfriend. Eventually, as I had sensed all along, the transition happened months later!"

Lessons on Change

These experiences taught me that change is inevitable and often necessary for growth. Transitions can be daunting, but they also hold opportunities for transformation. While my teenage self-resisted preparation, I now see the value in equipping ourselves and our children for the seasons of life.

How to Embrace Transitions

As believers, we can navigate transitions with faith and resilience. Here's how:

Prayer and Reflection

God has been so kind to me. Often, He speaks to me before different seasons in my life, and I have sometimes honestly not been attuned. We need to seek God's guidance through regular prayer. Reflect on what the transition teaches you and how it aligns with His plan for your life.

Meditation on Scripture

Anchor yourself in God's promises. Meditate on the word, letting it fill your heart and form your thoughts.

Learn what God plans for you and find hope and purpose in Him.

Community Support

Surround yourself with a supportive network of believers. Sharing your experiences with others provides strength and encouragement during challenging transitions.

Embrace Uncertainty

Understand that uncertainty is part of growth. Trust that God is in control and that every season serves a purpose.

Look for Opportunities

Transitions often open doors to new experiences, relationships, and growth. Stay open to how God may be leading you.

Practice Gratitude

Focus on the positives, even during difficult transitions. The Bible encourages us to give thanks in all circumstances, trusting that God works all things for our good.

Boundaries

As someone who has often found myself emotionally overwhelmed in relationships and friendships simply because I didn't establish boundaries, I've realized how vital it is to set and define boundaries in all types of relationships. As Pastor Stephanie Ike says, boundaries are for protection. I truly believe they are fundamental! It's equally important that we teach our children how to set boundaries.

Many of us, like I was today, find ourselves struggling emotionally, in the wrong places, hurting, feeling betrayed, unloved, or even used all because we didn't set boundaries. Pastor Stephanie Ike also says that boundaries are formed on foundations, and the strength of any building depends on the strength of its foundation. Walls of protection are built on a firm foundation.

Parents, your children need to be firmly built with the values you want them to uphold for the rest of their lives. Teach them now. Instil the principles and actions they should take in specific situations or when encountering certain people. The Bible reminds us: *"Direct your children onto the right path, and when they are older, they will not leave it" (Proverbs 22:6, NLT).*

However, many parents, especially in some cultures, miss the opportunity to explicitly teach children about relationships, friendships, and how to interact with the opposite gender. Instead, we hear vague warnings like, "Men are evil," "Women are dangerous," or "Men are dogs." As a result, many of us grew up waiting for these "dogs" to appear, only to "find well-meaning, good-looking, and sometimes even God-fearing people".

Believing we were safe, we settled in. But over time, sometimes, after wasting precious time, we realized things weren't what they seemed. Worse, we discovered this while already hurting, used, or abandoned. The issue often lies in undefined boundaries.

I've learned that boundaries are personal. You set them based on who you are, what you believe, and what you will or won't tolerate. Then, depending on the person or situation, you can tighten those boundaries as needed.

Having clearly defined values is key. Remember, the Bible says: "But I am not surprised! Even Satan disguises himself as an angel of light" *(2 Corinthians 11:14, NLT).*

The devil doesn't come dressed in obvious signs of evil. He's crafty. But if you are submitted to the Lord, you can resist him.

If you are confident in who you are, know what you want, and have firm boundaries, you can save yourself from heartache and wasted time. I learned this the hard way, but you don't have to. Let's take the time to understand and implement boundaries in our lives.

Understanding Boundaries in Relationships

Boundaries in relationships are the guidelines, rules, or limits people establish to protect their well-being and ensure healthy interactions. They promote mutual respect, trust, and understanding.

Types of Boundaries

- Physical Boundaries relate to personal space, physical touch, and privacy. For example, "I'm not comfortable with hugging strangers."

- Emotional Boundaries: Protect your emotional well-being by managing how much you share and how you handle others' emotions. Example: "I need time to process my feelings before we discuss this."

- Time Boundaries: Respect each other's time and priorities. Example: "I can't meet tonight; I've already committed to other plans."

- Intellectual Boundaries: Respect each other's ideas, beliefs, and opinions. Example: "I value your perspective, but I don't agree with that."

- Financial Boundaries: Set limits on spending, saving, or sharing money. Example: "I'm

comfortable splitting expenses, but I prefer to keep our finances separate."
- Digital Boundaries: Manage privacy and behavior in the digital space. For example, "Please don't share my photos without asking."

Why Boundaries Are Important

- Promote mutual respect and prevent resentment.
- Help maintain individuality within a relationship.
- Prevent feelings of being overwhelmed, used, or controlled.
- Foster open communication and understanding.

How to Set Boundaries

- Identify Your Needs: Reflect on what makes you uncomfortable.
- Communicate Clearly: Be assertive and direct without being confrontational. For example, "I need some alone time after work to recharge."
- Be Consistent: Enforce your boundaries consistently to avoid confusion.
- Respect Others' Boundaries: Recognize that others also have their limits.
- Evaluate and Adjust: Reassess boundaries as relationships grow or circumstances change.

Red Flags of Poor Boundaries
- Feeling guilty for saying "no."
- Overcommitting or neglecting your needs.
- Accepting disrespectful behavior.
- Having unclear expectations, leading to misunderstandings.

By setting and respecting boundaries, we protect ourselves and those we care about from unnecessary pain and disappointment. Let's make this a priority for ourselves and the next generation!

Conclusion: Navigating Life's Changes with Faith

Life is a series of transitions, joyful and painful but all meaningful. Embracing change requires faith, courage, and a willingness to grow. While we can't always predict what's ahead, being attuned to God's voice and trusting His promise that He will never leave or forsake us will keep us steadfast. Transitions may be inevitable, but with God as our anchor, we can face them with hope and resilience.

Family relationships, while precious, are not without their challenges. Misunderstandings, unspoken pain, and generational wounds often strain the bonds we hold dear. Healing these relationships requires forgiveness, an act that is both difficult and transformative. Forgiveness is a powerful bridge to restoration, freeing us from bitterness and creating space for love to thrive.

> "Single mothers, never lose hope. The Lord God is your redeemer, and you should see yourselves as He sees you."
> -Evelin Viera at Photizo Daily

CHAPTER FOURTEEN

FORGIVENESS

"Forgiveness is one of the most beautiful words in the human vocabulary. How much pain and unhappy consequences could be avoided if we all learned the meaning of this word."
–Billy Graham

Forgiveness is one of the hardest conversations to have, especially if you've endured deep pain. I will admit I am no expert on this. I have had to wrestle with it and bring it before the Holy Spirit, asking Him to open my heart and give me understanding. Each hurt requires its own approach.

I have found healing for some wounds over time; as the saying goes, "time heals." Sometimes, I have cried out to God and let it go, yet others, it just took a great conversation with a trusted person. One thing God has strongly spoken to me for us concerning this book is that He wants to heal.

Many of us struggle in this area because pain, for the longest time, has become our identity; strife has become a part of us that we cannot imagine being without it. That is not what God wants for us; He wants us to live in freedom. And sometimes, it will get us out of our comfort zone.

Sometimes, some struggle because they are afraid to start over again, not knowing what to expect. But I loved what my pastor once said: **"Obedience does not look at the outcome."**

We must trust God with the outcome because He commands us to forgive. I also know that some of us struggle because of pride, yet forgiveness is indispensable regardless of what it is.

The Meaning of Forgiveness

One of the Greek words for forgiveness is "aphiemi," which means "to let go, to release." It means to be free and release someone. I always thought I had forgiven, but I was still carrying so much pain. One person had hurt me so profoundly that the burden of that pain lingered for almost three years. It was unbearable.

Then, one day, God revealed something so simple yet transformative: He said, just as He had forgiven me of all my sins, He had forgiven that other person, too. I was both angry and amazed. Like some of you, I always wondered why God would so easily let go of such. But He is God, all-powerful yet so merciful.

This realization changed everything for me. Understanding that God extends the same mercy and grace to them as He does to me was humbling. If God Himself does not hold their sins against them, who am I to do so? I let it go and treated them like they didn't do what they did.

Forgiveness as Dying to Self

Forgiveness isn't just about letting go of the pain; it is about dying to self. Once, I was invited to a party during a season when I felt hurt and betrayed. I went with the only friend who had been by my side.

When we arrived, I unexpectedly encountered the person who had caused me pain from the start. I passed them like I had not seen them, but my friend stopped to greet them! I was so upset, not only because I had met someone I did not want and planned to meet but also because my friend chose to act differently. I felt betrayed. hahaha.

But that is not what the Bible teaches us. Forgiveness means surrendering your pride, sense of justice, and right to hold onto anger. We must continually exchange our will for God's will. Through prayer, I continually surrendered that individual to God. Over time, my heart began to clear, but it did not mean everything returned to how it was.

I have learned that forgiveness does not always mean close association. Sometimes, the relationship does not return to its original closeness, and that's okay. Forgiveness means releasing the burden of pain and entrusting the situation to God, but it does not necessarily mean reinstating someone to the same position in your life.

The Role of God's Servants in My Healing

During my journey, Joyce Meyer's and Joel Osteen's teachings were instrumental in helping me find clarity. I love their teachings! They often speak about the mind and soul, where much of the struggle with forgiveness occurs.

Joyce Meyer's words especially touched a nerve: *"When you trust God, you must do good."* This teaching is rooted in Psalms 37:3 KJV, *"Trust in the Lord, and do good; so shalt thou dwell in the land, and verily thou shalt be fed."*

It reminded me of the call to love our enemies, which many scriptures say in the New Testament. That is unreasonable and impossible for us as human beings when we have been deeply hurt, but it is possible when we wholly trust God to help us. Joyce Meyer's teaching provoked me and gave me the courage to align my actions with my faith, even when I did not feel like it.

Another pivotal moment came during a prayer leaders' meeting at church. The topic of forgiveness unexpectedly arose, and I was overwhelmed with emotion. Someone I deeply trusted had caused me immense pain in that season, and I was still reeling from the betrayal. In tears, I asked the group, **"What does forgiveness mean?"**

Different leaders shared their thoughts, and while their words brought some relief, the answers felt incomplete. The following day, God used my pastor, Tom Kiessling, to deliver a full teaching on forgiveness. That teaching became a turning point, offering me the clarity and peace I desperately needed. God always sends His word to me at the right time and has healed my heart.

Forgiveness Comes with Wisdom

One of the most freeing truths I have learned is that forgiveness does not mean you have to give someone the same place in your life.

People often ask me how I handle those who hurt me, and my response is simple: "I deal with wisdom." This did not come easy; I had to learn it.

For a long time, I was in cycles of the same things I suffered before because I forgave but still had no boundaries. I know some of us suffer from this, entertaining the same people who are doing the same things to us and expecting different results. I know this is relative, but it is not selfish to choose how you want to deal with someone who has abused you. I love space, and I have learned to give it to those who need and deserve it.

Forgiveness means letting go of the pain and acknowledging that if Jesus forgave them, I have no right to hold onto resentment. But it does not mean entrusting them with the same level of closeness or responsibility. Forgiveness and trust are two different things. While forgiveness is given freely, trust is earned; it must be rebuilt.

The Power of Letting Go

If you're struggling with pain from someone's actions, I encourage you to find the strength to let it go. Forgiveness isn't about excusing what happened or pretending the pain isn't real. It is about releasing yourself from the weight of bitterness and allowing God to heal your heart.

I have found that when I still feel pain, it is often a sign that I haven't fully released the hurt. Forgiveness is a process that takes time, prayer, and a willingness to let God work in your heart. Forgiveness is less about the other person and more about your freedom. Choose to let go, not because they deserve it, but because you do. I live freely!

I Took Back My Power

The journey to healing and forgiveness is far from linear; it is messy, layered, and often painful. While I have made progress, I know I'm still navigating this process.

Delays in releasing this book stemmed from my fears; I have been playing it safe, but not anymore: How would people perceive me? How would those who caused my deepest wounds react? What about the judgment from those who will misunderstand my story? These fears weighed heavily on me, but not anymore.

Silence is golden, but how long shall we stay silent concerning what we suffer? Why should your children suffer the same things you have suffered simply because you are afraid of being judged or scared to be vulnerable? I refuse!

I have learned to extend grace to myself, be kind and patient with my journey, and embrace my story. Before speaking on specific topics, I used to think I needed certain milestones, such as marriage or a child. I wanted to avoid criticism like, "What does she know about this?" But I have realized that waiting to be "qualified" was holding me back from obeying God. Even the Apostle Paul did not need to be married to speak profound truths about relationships. Obedience, not perfection, matters, and this book is part of my obedience to God.

Harder Lessons from Unhealthy Relationships

One of my greatest struggles has been setting healthy boundaries, particularly with men. I have found myself drawn to emotionally unavailable people, seeking validation from those who did not genuinely love, respect, or value me. I stayed in relationships that drained me emotionally, holding onto the hope that things would change. But the truth is, I was afraid to let go because I did not know who I was without those attachments.

Healing isn't passive. It is deliberate. If you do not take intentional steps, you'll remain stuck in the same cycles of pain. I carried the wounds of my second relationship for years, regretting how long I stayed, knowing from the start that it was hopeless. The red flags were there, but my desperation for love blinded me. I endured abuse, believing that if I stayed long enough, love and marriage would follow. I was wrong. The relationship was toxic, and each day brought new arguments and deeper wounds.

One day, I reached my breaking point. Angry with myself for settling for so little, I decided to walk away. It was not easy. It cost me emotionally and financially, but it was one of the best choices I have ever made. I share this not to diminish your pain but to assure you that freedom is possible. You must pursue it. God's mercy carried me through. I am a testimony that you can heal from all sorts of abuse.

The Cost of Suppressed Pain

Unaddressed pain is dangerous. It breeds bitterness, mistrust, and fear. I know this firsthand. For years, I carried so much hurt that it began to manifest in ways that even shocked me. I have been suicidal, withdrew from people, built more defensive walls, and convinced myself I was better off alone or even dead. At my lowest, I even wished I could numb the pain completely. But God held me together.

When someone new entered my life, I hesitantly shared again, allowing myself to feel hopeful. Yet, with time, I quickly realized I was bringing unresolved pain into this new connection. I became overly attached, obsessive, and controlling. The problem was not just them; it was me. I hadn't fully healed, and I was using the relationship as a bandage for wounds that needed deeper care.

True healing isn't always found in another person. It starts with confronting your pain. Recognize it and get to the heart of it. Healing does not mean perfection; it is about progress.

Confronting Anger and Finding Freedom

Ironically, one of the reasons I ended my first relationship was my partner's anger. Their short temper led to constant fights, and I eventually walked away. But in my second relationship, I realized that I had developed anger issues. Was it something I carried from the first relationship, or did the second one bring out the worst in me? Either way, I knew I needed to deal with it.

I brought my anger before God, cried it out with fasting, and prayed for healing. While time played a role, I have understood that true healing comes from God. As I surrendered my pain, I began to feel whole again. I realized I had been giving people too much power over me, but forgiveness and healing helped me reclaim it.

Forgiveness and healing go hand in hand. When you hold onto bitterness, you remain a prisoner to those who hurt you. Letting go does not mean forgetting; it means freeing yourself.

Reclaiming My Power

One of the most significant moments in my journey came when someone from my past tried to manipulate me again. This time, I said, "No." That single word may seem small, but it was monumental for someone who once struggled with boundaries. When they asked again, I smiled wider and repeated, "No." At that moment, my heart whispered, ***"I took back my power."***

Healing allows you to make choices for yourself not out of fear, guilt, or obligation but from a place of freedom.

Taking Back Your Power

Taking back your power starts with becoming self-aware and taking responsibility for your healing. Let go of bitterness. Forgive those who hurt you not because they deserve it but because you deserve peace.

Stop letting others control your emotions and reclaim the freedom that is rightfully yours. You are worth it. You are capable of healing, and you can take back your power, one deliberate step at a time.

Forgiveness is a deeply personal process that frees us from the weight of bitterness and pain, allowing us to move forward with grace and peace. Yet, the healing journey often calls us to put our reflections and emotions into words.

Writing letters is a powerful way to confront, release, or express gratitude. As we end this book, I share some personal letters I have written on my behalf and on behalf of those with similar experiences and situations as discussed in the chapters (to) the concerned.

CHAPTER FIFTEEN

LETTERS OF THE HEART TO AND FROM THE CONCERNED

Dear Mom,
I have been thinking a lot lately about some things that have been hard for me to understand fully. You've always wanted the best for me and protected me in many ways. I love you for that and am grateful for everything you've done. But there is something that's been in my heart that I need to talk about: the fact that you kept me from my dad.
I realize you probably had your reasons, and maybe you felt it was best for me or even necessary. I do not know what you've been through, and I know things between you and Dad may have been complicated or painful. But growing up without him has left me with a lot of questions, confusion, and feelings I do not always know how to process.
I missed having a relationship with him, and even though I do not know the full story, I can't help but wonder what might have been different if I had known him. I'm not angry at you, but I feel hurt and sad. It is hard not to think about the times I could have spent with him and the memories that were never made. In the meantime, can you get me a father figure to help me answer some of my questions? Can you get me a therapist?
I want you to know that I do not blame you, but I need to understand why things happened the way they did. I want to know the truth, even if it is painful. I hope we can talk about it one day so I can have some clarity and maybe even some peace.
No matter what, I love you and know you did what you thought was best for me. I need to hear your side and work through some of my feelings. I hope we can have that conversation because it will help me heal. Thank you for always

being there for me, and I hope you can understand where I'm coming from.

With love,
   Your Teenager/Young Adult

Dear Mom/Dad,
   I know that I haven't always acted the way I should, and I want to take a moment to apologize for the times I misbehaved or hurt you. It hasn't been easy for me to admit this, but I need you to know that a lot of my actions came from a place of pain and confusion, not because I wanted to hurt you or make things harder.
   I have gone through things that I haven't always known how to deal with. They feel like they have been bottled up inside me, and sometimes, the only way they come out is through anger, frustration, or acting out. I wish I could have handled things differently, but in those moments, I did not know how to process everything I felt.
   I know that's no excuse, and I take responsibility for my choices. But I also hope you can understand that what you saw was not truly who I am; I struggled with things I did not know how to express. I have been hurting, and instead of asking for help, I let that pain show in ways that weren't fair to you or anyone else.
   I'm working on healing, learning how to face what's happened and grow beyond it. I need to communicate better and be more open about what's happening inside me, and I'm trying to improve at that. I want a healthier relationship with you, built on understanding and trust rather than miscommunication or acting out.
   I appreciate your patience, even when I did not deserve it. I love you, and I'm sorry for the times I let my pain hurt you. I hope

we can work through this together, and I'm open to having honest conversations if you are willing.

With love,
Your Child

Dear Single mom/dad,
    I want to take a moment to acknowledge the incredible strength and love you show as a single mom/dad. Being raised by a single mother, I know firsthand how much it takes to balance everything, such as raising a child, providing for them, and giving them the best life possible. I want you to know that your sacrifices and hard work do not go unnoticed, and they have a lasting impact. I am here by the Grace of God and my mom, who just like you, took up the responsibility of being a mother, and did not desert us.
    Growing up, I saw my mom do everything she could to care for us. I know it must have been overwhelming for her sometimes, and I'm sure you feel the weight of it, too. But through her love, I also saw the hand of God at work. He provided, even when it seemed like we did not have enough. He gave my mom the strength to keep going, and I know He will do the same for you.
    As a child raised by a single mom, I can tell you that the love and devotion you pour into your child will shape them in powerful ways. You are teaching them resilience, strength, and faith lessons that will stay with them forever. I am everything my mom taught me with words and deeds. Her faith carried us through hard times, inspiring me to trust God more deeply.
    I know there are days when it feels too much, and you might wonder if you're doing enough. But I want to remind you that God sees everything you're doing. He is with you during every sleepless night, decision, and every tear you cry. As Isaiah 41:10 NIV says, "Do not fear, for I am with you; do not be dismayed, for I am your God. I will strengthen you and help you; I will uphold

you with my righteous right hand." You are not alone on this journey. God is with you, and He will sustain you.

Your child is blessed to have you as their mom or dad. Don't hesitate to find support. You are thriving this season, and God is proud of you. Keep trusting Him and know that your love and commitment are making a difference in your child's life, just as my mom's did in mine.

With love and prayers,
 Vivienne, Maama Photizo.

Dear Pastors,

I can't mention all your names, but I love and thank God for many of you. I want to take a moment to express my deep appreciation for the work you do and the impact you've had on my life. The absence of my dad left a significant void in my heart and my understanding of who I was. It was a painful reality that shaped much of my childhood, but coming to church changed the trajectory of my life through your teaching, patience, kindness, and unwavering love for me and many like me.

Thank you for being fathers to those of us who never experienced the love, protection, or guidance of an earthly dad. Your presence, wisdom, and how you model Christ's love have made all the difference.

Thank you for being anchors in our lives and not giving up on us. I know some of us are crazier than others. Thank you for pointing us to God's love and for helping us understand that our values and identity are rooted in Him. I know some of you have adopted some of us and provided shelter, food, and education. Your impact is immeasurable; your ministry has been a source of healing, restoration, and hope for me. Please do not grow weary in your service towards many like me; God is your reward.

With deep gratitude,
 Vivienne, Maama Photizo

ENDLESS QUEST

Dear Family Members

I hope this letter finds you well. I am writing to extend my heartfelt thoughts and prayers as your family navigates the challenges of caring for [Orphan's Name]. I understand this can be overwhelming, but I want you to know you are not alone.

Caring for a child who has lost their parents is a profound responsibility, but it is also an incredible opportunity to offer love, stability, and hope. Your kindness and compassion during this time will shape their future in ways that are beyond measure. While financial support is certainly important, it is essential to recognize that [Orphan's Name] needs far more than just physical provisions.

Psychologically, a child who has experienced such loss is often dealing with deep grief, confusion, and insecurity. They need consistent emotional support to help them navigate these feelings. This means offering a patient ear when they are ready to talk, being observant of changes in their behavior, and providing reassurance that they are safe and loved.

The Bible reminds us of our responsibility to stand up for children and those in need: Psalm 82:3 NIV says, "Defend the weak and the fatherless; uphold the cause of the poor and the oppressed." Children, especially orphans, need the security of knowing that they are loved and protected. They need guidance, understanding, and patience to help them make sense of their loss and feel safe in the new world they are living in.

Spiritually, this is a critical time for [Orphan's Name] to develop a relationship with God. As they process their loss, they may question life, faith, and why such things happen. Offering them spiritual guidance, helping them understand that God is always with them, and introducing them to prayer can give them a strong foundation. Scripture assures us that He is a father to the fatherless. It is important to show [Orphan's Name] that, although their earthly parents are no longer with them, they have a heavenly Father who will never abandon them.

However, if children in these circumstances are not attended to thoroughly, especially psychologically, emotionally, and spiritually, the impacts can be severe. Without emotional support, children may struggle with feelings of abandonment, anger, and anxiety. They could face long-term issues such as trust difficulties, attachment problems, or low self-esteem. These children need to know they are valued and their emotions matter.

Spiritually, neglecting their growth can lead to a lack of purpose or even bitterness toward God. They might grow distant from their faith, feeling abandoned or lost. However, with proper spiritual nurturing, they can develop a strong sense of hope, resilience, and peace that will sustain them throughout their life. It is crucial that [Orphan's Name] receives balanced care of mind, body, and spirit.

Establishing a healthy routine, open communication, and involvement in a supportive faith community can help them thrive. Encourage their spiritual growth through prayer, Bible reading, and involvement in church community for children and youth, and remind them of God's unfailing love. As Proverbs 22:6 NLT says, "Direct your children onto the right path, and when they are older, they will not leave it."

This investment in their emotional and spiritual well-being will have lasting impacts beyond childhood. Please know that you do not have to bear this burden alone. Help and support are available from family, friends, the church, and other resources. I pray for strength, wisdom, and peace to guide you through this time.

With love and prayers,
 Vivienne, Maama Photizo

Dear toxic parent,

I hope this letter finds you well. I am reaching out to you sincerely for understanding and healing. As someone who understands what it means to feel rejected by your parents yet values and believes in compassion, forgiveness, and reconciliation, I feel compelled to address the pain and hurt that has come from the relationship between you and your child. .

I am aware that the past between you and your child has been fraught with pain and hardship. The impact of rejection or abuse is profound and lasting. However, I also believe in the possibility of healing and change. It is important to acknowledge the hurt that has occurred and to take responsibility for it. This is a step towards making amends and a path to personal growth and renewal in your relationship with God.

Your child deserves to know they are valued and loved and that the past does not define their worth. They also deserve to see that you are willing to acknowledge your mistakes and work towards making things right. This process may be challenging, but it is a testament to your commitment to personal growth and the well-being of your family.

I pray you find the strength and wisdom to seek your child's forgiveness and repair and rebuild your relationship. I pray you find the courage to reach out with an open heart and seek reconciliation. May you find guidance and support in this journey, and may you and your child find healing and peace.

I want to remind you of God's grace and love's transformative nature. It is never too late to seek redemption and to strive for a better future. I pray that you take this opportunity to reflect deeply and act with compassion and sincerity.

With sincere hope and prayers for healing,
   Vivienne, Maama Photizo

Dear abused child/woman/man

I am deeply sorry for the pain you endured at the hands of someone who should have loved, protected, and nurtured you. The rejection/abuse you experienced are wounds that no one should ever have to carry. I cannot fully understand the depth of your suffering, but I want to encourage you with a message of hope, love, and healing.

As a follower of Christ, I believe in the transforming power of His love. Though people in this world may fail us, God never does. Psalm 27:10 NLT says, "Even if my father and mother abandon me, the LORD will hold me close." You are not alone in your pain. God sees you, knows you, and desires to bring healing to the broken places in your heart.

Jesus Himself understands what it means to be rejected. He came into this world full of love and was despised, rejected, and even crucified by those He came to save. But through His suffering, He made a way for us to experience true freedom, peace, and reconciliation. No matter what has been done to you, God offers the grace to heal and restore.

Forgiveness may seem impossible, and I do not want to minimize what you've been through. But as you lean on God, He will give you the strength to release the burden of bitterness, allowing you to walk in freedom. Ephesians 4:31-32, NLT reminds us, "Get rid of all bitterness, rage, anger, harsh words, slander, and all types of evil behavior. Instead, be kind to each other, tenderhearted, forgiving one another, just as God through Christ has forgiven you..." Forgiveness does not excuse what happened; it sets you free.

You are precious in God's eyes, and the actions of others do not define your worth. You are His beloved child, wonderfully made and deeply cherished. As you walk this healing journey, know that God is with you every step. He can turn your mourning into dancing, ashes into beauty, and sorrow into joy.

I will continue to pray that you may feel the depth of God's love, experience His peace that surpasses all understanding, and be comforted by His presence. May He lead you beside still waters, restore your soul, and heal every wound.

With love in Christ,
    Vivienne, Maama Photizo

Dear Men,
   I write this letter with a heavy heart, hoping to speak truth and light into a serious issue. From my experience, observation, and study, I see that many young girls are vulnerable and hurtful, searching for love, guidance, and protection from father figures. Unfortunately, some men take advantage of their innocence and desperation. As a follower of Christ, I must address this issue with love, urgency, and honesty because I have experienced it.
   Exploiting a young woman who is seeking a brother/friend, or a father figure is not just an act of betrayal; it is a deep violation of trust and innocence. These girls are often wounded, looking for a sense of security, and instead, they are left with deeper scars. They were not created to be used but to be cherished and protected. These girls and women are precious and worthy of dignity and respect.

   Matthew 18:6 NLT says, "But if you cause one of these little ones who trusts in me to fall into sin, it would be better for you to have a large millstone tied around your neck and be drowned in the depths of the sea." This verse shows how seriously God views the protection of the vulnerable.
   Sometimes, just like me for a long time, many do not even know what they seek. What you may see as a temporary satisfaction is leaving a lasting impact on these girls, affecting their self-worth, emotional well-being, and future relationships. You may not fully understand the damage caused, but they carry it with them, often for years. Jesus teaches us to love, protect, and serve others, not to take advantage of them for selfish gain.

Exploiting the vulnerable goes against everything God calls us to as believers.

There is, however, hope for change. Jesus Christ offers forgiveness and a new life in Him. He gives us the power to turn from destructive ways. If you've been using your influence in ways that harm others, I encourage you to repent. Turn away from this path, seek God's forgiveness, and walk in integrity and righteousness.

God designed men as protectors, leaders, and examples of His love. The young girls seeking a father figure seek safety, guidance, and care, which can only be given in purity and wisdom. You can be that source of strength, reflect God's heart as a loving father, and build up instead of tear down. Please consider the weight of your actions. It is not too late to choose a new path that leads to life and healing for you and the young souls you encounter. God is calling you to be a man of honor, to lift the brokenhearted, and to provide the love and stability these young girls need. I pray that you find the courage to walk in truth and righteousness and begin to see the value in living a life that honors God and protects the vulnerable.

In Christ,
Vivienne, Maama Photizo

Dear society,

I am writing as someone whose dad was absent, knows and understands childhood trauma, and though I have grown, the effects have lingered into my adult life. Trauma shapes us in ways that aren't always visible. I have wrestled with pain, confusion, and questions about why things happened the way they did.

Yet, I have come to realize that God was always with me. Psalm 46:1 NIV says, "God is our refuge and strength, an ever-present help in trouble." I have found strength and comfort in Him, but healing is not something we can do alone. There have been some remarkable people in my life, and I want to thank those of you who have been kind to me and others with my experience.

I am aware that sometimes society labels children who've been through trauma as "trouble," "angry," or "difficult," but what we need is your understanding. As someone who has been judged continuously by people who know nothing about me, I would gladly ask you always to know people's stories before you make conclusions about them. God calls us compassionate and bear one another's burdens (Galatians 6:2).

Trauma does not define us; we can overcome it with God's love and support from the community. Healing requires empathy and a willingness to see beyond the behavior to the pain beneath.

I ask you to see us as more than our pasts or reactions. With God's grace, we can rise above trauma, but we need people who reflect His love and care. Please, be that reflection. With your understanding, we can find healing and hope.

Sincerely,
Vivienne, Maama Photizo

Living a Life That Writes Its Own Story

Just like my sister does not agree with me on some things I have shared, kindly know that it is okay if you've found things you do not fully agree with. I'm just glad you've read this far. My sister played a big role in helping me write out some of these experiences, which some friends who were kind enough to share but could not write and decided to share their stories by sending me WhatsApp audios. My big sister put in countless hours to help transcribe these, and I want to give her a big shout-out! My prayer is that she'll eventually read my book. hahaha.

I wouldn't want anyone to be like the 16-year-old me. Instead of reading the book that, in hindsight, God sent me through a friend, I felt stumbled and offended. I'm not sure how you feel right now or where you are as a father, mother, or child, but I pray that we all grasp the bigger picture of everything I have shared. Dr. Myles Munroe says there is no such thing as a "personal life" if you truly have character. As someone whose name has been tarnished by people spreading false things, I'd rather be the one to tell my story.

One thing that always humbles me is death; at funerals, you hear stories you would never imagine a person was part of. It reminds me of a quote I once saw: **"Live well so we do not have to lie at your funeral."** I say, tell your story and live it so it speaks for itself and lives on when you're gone.

Shout-out to all the courageous people who have shared their stories; their lives truly attest to the need for fathers, as I have expressed throughout this book.

EPILOGUE 1

IMPACT OF DADS THROUGH MY FRIENDS' EYES

Sylvia Katusiime-Uganda.

When it comes to my daddy, words are never enough. Apart from the love of Jesus, I have never known a man's love like that of my earthly father. From the many impromptu school visits, solo car drives, and choir rehearsals in our living room, my father was always my favorite company.

Even when I messed up at school or home, he was there to validate my feelings and lovingly correct me. He was my number one cheerleader, protector, confidant, and greatest love!

Our relationship made it easy for me to communicate with my Father in heaven because my earthly father was a direct example of God's desire to connect with us. I always felt a sense of confidence, importance, security, and belonging because of my dad's presence. His love showed me exactly how a man should treat me, he set the standard. Though he left too soon, I believe the impact of his presence during my early years has shaped the person I am today. I'll always be my daddy's little girl. May his precious soul continue to rest eternally.

Cassie Comfort, MA, USA.

I did not realize how much growing up without a father had impacted my life until I met my husband. He would point out that, at times, I was disrespectful toward him, and I did not even notice it. He told me I gave off this masculine, "I do not need a man" kind of energy. Then, he asked if I grew up with my father, and when I said no, he suggested that might explain some of my behavior.

Growing up, I realized I lacked male guidance and a father figure's authority. I was used to doing everything myself because I had always known that. With time, I had to look deeper into myself and explore the root of my behavior. I'm trying to work on it, though I can still get defensive.

Counsel George Tumwine, Uganda
Son of Mr. George Byaruhanga.

Growing up with my father present and actively involved in my life profoundly impacted my Christian faith and development as a man. His presence provided a tangible model of God's love, patience, and guidance. Through his actions and teachings, I learned the importance of integrity, responsibility, and humility, which he likely gained from his work and church, central to Christianity and the body of Christ. My father provided for my physical needs and nurtured my spiritual growth.

He prayed with me and encouraged me to seek God in all circumstances. I still remember when he taught me John 3:16 one evening during my primary school days, sowing seeds of the truth that Christ died for our sins and loved us unconditionally. To this day, I carry that verse in my heart as a constant reminder of Christ's sacrifice and love. His life mirrored the teachings of Christ, showing me how to live out my faith daily as I later became a man serving God and the legal profession.

Moreover, my father's availability meant I always had someone to turn to for advice and support in my spiritual journey.

Whether helping me understand the Bible or guiding me through moral dilemmas, he was always there, offering wisdom grounded in Scripture. His consistent guidance deepened my understanding of God as a loving Father who is always present, offering grace and direction. My father's example helped shape my relationship with Christ, as I witnessed firsthand the power of living a life rooted in faith, love, and service to others.

Bwogi John, cousin, Uganda.

Growing up with my old man was normal. Like all good fathers, he tried his best to provide for his family. I can't say he was perfect because no one is perfect, but he tried his best, I guess.

Chorm Cathy, Nairobi, Kenya:

Growing up with my dad, there was always a profound sense of safety and security whenever he was home. His presence was like a shield, a promise of protection. Unlike other kids in the neighborhood, we were never sent on errands by neighbors; everyone knew that our dad did not tolerate anyone messing with his children. Dad was also a master of provision. I always believed that he would find a way to ensure we were cared for. His determination was unwavering, and he never failed to provide for us, no matter the challenge.

One of the most powerful lessons he taught me was to fight for my life. I witnessed his battle with cancer for two years, a fight marked by relentless strength and resilience. Despite the odds and the dire situation at Mulago Cancer Institute, a government hospital with scarce resources, Dad was determined to get on the doctors' list and secure a bed. Even in his weakened state, he fought to make things easier for me as his caretaker, demonstrating his unyielding spirit.

Love was another area where Dad's actions spoke volumes. Despite the tough-love approach often seen in our culture, I always felt his gentleness. Whenever he noticed I was in a bad mood, he would softly ask, *"Kyomukama, are you okay?"* His tenderness was a constant reassurance. Above all, Dad's trust in me shaped who I am today. He believed in my potential and allowed me to make my own choices. His support for my decisions was unwavering, instilling a deep self-belief.

———◆◇◆———

Apostle Samuel Mulindwa Tebandeke, MA, USADad: Pastor Fredrick Mulindwa.

A present father is not just defined by his physical proximity but by his ability to lead and guide his family, even from miles away. My experience growing up is a testament to this. Though my Mzee spent much of his time in the States while we were back home, his presence was undeniably felt.

We knew better than to misbehave because whenever my mother said, "I'm going to tell your dad when he calls," it struck fear in us. And when Mzee would say over the phone, "When I come back in December, I'll deal with you," we believed him.

The mere thought of his return was enough to keep us in line. In a way, we were raised to fear God; in the same breath, we feared our father's discipline. But this fear kept us grounded and respectful, shaping us into disciplined individuals. My mother managed the household daily but did so with my father's authority backing her up. She was not just holding things together but reinforcing his leadership even when he was thousands of miles away.

What made my dad a great father was not his perfection but his constant presence, both emotional and authoritative. He remained connected to us even from afar, leading the family with a strong hand. To this day, his influence still shapes us. He may not have been perfect, but he was always there in the most important ways. His ability to lead from a distance, instill discipline, and stay connected with his family despite the miles is a true mark of a present father.

Judith Trish, Uganda.

I grew up in a blended family, surrounded by a diverse and loving household. Before my parents met, my mother had two children, and my father had one. Together, they had five more, making a total of eight siblings.

As a child, I didn't fully understand the dynamics of my family, but the signs were always there. My paternal sister, for instance, was always a bit of a loner with a tough exterior that hid her vulnerability. In contrast, my maternal siblings seemed to fit in, effortlessly navigating our family's complexities.

As I grew older, I began to appreciate the unique roles both mothers and fathers play interchangeably in a child's life. A mother's influence is often evident, as she is typically the primary caregiver. However, a father's presence is equally vital, providing a distinct kind of support and guidance that shapes a child's self-esteem and identity. In my case, I was fortunate to have both parents present and involved in my life.

My father was the disciplinarian, while my mother was the nurturer, always cuddling us until she wasn't, and I learned to appreciate the complexities of her role. I was blessed to start my own family last year, and early this year, I had a child. Now, I truly understand the value of a father's presence. My husband, raised by a single mother, had a vastly different experience. Despite having both parents around, his father was largely absent, leaving his mother to shoulder all, if not most, of the responsibilities.

As a result, my husband had to navigate the challenges of adolescence without the guidance of a father. He moved out of the family home at 14, claiming he was old enough! Maybe it would be a different story now if the father had been more involved. The emotional scars are evident as a father himself, and he is a bit too determined to break the cycle of absentee fatherhood. He is deeply involved in our daughter's life, proudly showcasing her to everyone he can and talking about her constantly.

While his enthusiasm can sometimes be overwhelming, and I understand the motivation behind it, sometimes I think he's simply trying to prove to himself that he is not his father, and it may be detrimental. My girl should enjoy her father and mother altogether, but I'm afraid it may snap when you strain something for too long and hard. I pray every day for God's grace, guidance, and patience.

Pastor Sandra N, MA, USA
Growing Up Without My Parents.

I lost my parents at such an early age that I do not even remember them. I have a faint memory of saying goodbye to my dad, who was seated in a wheelchair because he knew he was about to pass.

They sent us to live with my mom's sister and our aunt. I did not feel sad at that moment, but as I grew older, the memories started returning. I do not remember seeing my mom at all because I was told she died first. Both my parents passed away from HIV/AIDS before effective medicine was available.

Growing up, I did not realize the pain of not having parents until I became older. As I matured, I understood that we all need a support system. I won't say that the people who raised me did not do a good job; they did. But there was always a gap in my heart, a need for a friend I could confide in.

Now, I tell myself that there are things I could have learned from my mother's conversations that would have been special, topics I could never share with anyone else. I grew into a strong woman, knowing that God was the only one I had to lean on because I had no one else to run to. There isn't a day when memories of my mother do not fall back. Special days like Mother's Day bring tears to my eyes. Seeing everyone else celebrate their mothers makes me cry.

There is no Mother's Day. I haven't cried because the pain of not having her is still so real. But I thank God for the Holy Spirit, who comforts me. I would not know God the way I do if it weren't for losing my parents.

My relationship with the Holy Spirit is so strong now that nothing can separate us. I thank God that all things work together for good for those who love the Lord and are called according to His purpose. I would not be where I am today without Him and my trials. I'm truly a product of God's grace.

Phionah Sentongo- MA, USA
Growing Up Without My Dad.

I was told that my dad passed away when my mom was seven months pregnant with me. After I was born, my mom left the marriage and returned to her parents' home. So, growing up, I did not know anything about having a father until I was in second grade.

That's when I asked about him, and they told me he had passed away. I grew up with my grandmother, and every evening after school, I would ask about my dad. My grandma would always tell me the same thing: that he was away, that he had passed.

When I reached sixth grade, I visited my cousins and saw that they had a father. It warmed my heart, and I began to call him "Dad," too. I missed having my father so much. In high school, I had a friend with a dad, and I loved being around them. I always wanted to stay at their home to say "Daddy," too.

As I grew older and began to know God, I prayed for a man to be my husband, someone I could call "Daddy." Growing up in a home full of women, I did not realize a man was supposed to be in the house until I started living with my big sister, who had a husband.

When I met my husband, even before we had kids, I told him what I had always longed for. Seeing how he cared for and protected me was exciting; it was everything I had wished for. I pray for him always because he has been the "Daddy" I longed for, not just for me but also for our children. I pray God keeps us together. While it hurts to have an absent father, I know it is even more painful to have never seen him at all.

Maggie Nsamba, Uganda.
Growing up with a father is reassuring, comforting, and truly amazing. I have someone in my life who I can talk to about anything, no matter how shocking it may be.

I have someone who tells me straight if I'm being silly and whose judgment I can always trust to be true. My dad is full of compliments, very prayerful, and incredibly supportive. He is tough and gentle, always willing to offer a comforting hug when needed. He values prayer deeply.

Growing up, we had a family altar every night at 8 p.m., where we gathered to praise, worship, and pray to God. Each of us had a day or two every week to preach, which boosted our confidence and strengthened our trust in God. I feel incredibly privileged to have a father like mine.

Trina, Uganda.
Having my father by my side as I grew up was a gift that shaped me in countless ways. His presence was a constant reminder that I was loved, supported, and capable of achieving my dreams. He showed me what it

means to be a good person through his kindness, empathy, generosity, and how he treated and respected my mother.

His actions inspired me to follow in his footsteps. With his guidance, I learned to take risks, face my fears, and find my path. But it was not just me; my father's love and dedication extended to all of us.

He made sure we received a proper education, no matter the circumstances. Throughout our school years, he worked tirelessly to ensure we never lacked anything. His hard work and determination never wavered, even during the tough times.

I vividly remember when it was time for me to join the university. He told me it would not be possible because we did not have the money. I was heartbroken. But after seeing my reaction, he called me a few days later and told me to start looking for a hostel.

You can imagine how happy I was! That moment stays with me, a testament to his sacrifice and love. He celebrated my successes, helped me through my struggles, and was always there with a listening ear and a comforting word.

Looking back, I realize that his influence has been a constant source of strength, motivating me to become the best version of myself. I'm grateful for the memories we've made, the lessons he's taught me, and the unwavering support he has always provided.

I pray the Lord satisfies you with a long life, Taata Ssalongo Mujjasi Amedio.

Ronnie Omugabe–TX, USA
Growing Up with Dad.

Although my relationship with Dad was often marked more by fear than affection, especially during my teenage years, it has undoubtedly been one of the greatest influences shaping the man I am today. The excitement I felt as I rushed to grab his bags when he returned from his three-month work duties was immeasurable. The butterflies in my stomach when I handed him my report card and the smile across his face were priceless.

Those moments were always followed by what I now, as an adult, recognize as his affirmations of love: "I will make sure you study as far as you wish."

Throughout my childhood, I saw Dad face challenges and moments of lack, yet he never failed to fulfill his responsibilities as a father. I witnessed him lose his job, but I remained in school.

He later confided in me that he was under pressure every time I sat for exams, too, as though he were the one taking the tests. This only deepened my belief in the love I always knew he had for me. The desire to see Dad's smile when he read my report card pushed me to work even harder in school. Watching him work tirelessly year after year instilled in me a strong work ethic that my bosses appreciate today.

I easily embraced responsibility because I had watched Dad do the same for us, never wavering. Dad has taught me many of life's lessons, not through long speeches or counseling sessions, but by being an example of how he loved Mom as her husband and how he cared for us and his children.

Today, I can proudly say that my relationship with Dad has grown sweeter and stronger over the years, and I wholeheartedly thank God for the gift of a father like mine. Mr. Francis Tuhirirwe, thank you for your relentless love and unwavering commitment to your family without ever taking a break.

Winnie Mugagga–MA, USA
With Love and Appreciation to My Father.

My father, Mr. Katumba, came into my life at just the right time, during my teenage years, when guidance, understanding, and support were crucial. His presence provided me with a newfound sense of stability and direction. He stepped in as a figure of authority and as someone who deeply cared about my growth and well-being. Since then, he has been a grounding force in my life, whether physically by my side or not.

His influence is felt in the subtle, everyday moments, and his role has been significant in providing me with a sense of security, strength, and wisdom, shaping who I am today. His presence brings comfort, and his teachings and values guide me daily, reminding me of our deep bond.

Above all, he blessed me with two wonderful little sisters, Racheal and Deborah, who completely changed my world and gave me the cherished title of "big sister." For that, I am forever grateful.

Jane Namatovu, MA, USA.
My dad, my blessing, my inspiration, my hero, my safe place! It is a great privilege to talk about someone who has shaped my life in countless ways: my dad, friend, and

father. He is gentle yet strong, hardworking, and the true backbone of our home. He embodies what it means to be the priest of a household.

One story that stands out is from my first year on campus. In his relentless effort to provide for my education, he was tricked and robbed of everything he had worked for, all in the name of raising my tuition.

Sometimes, he walked in the rain and made and sold bricks to ensure my education was secured. How much more can a man give of himself? If you want to know what a responsible father looks like, I'll proudly show you mine.

One of the greatest lessons I have learned from my dad is the value of family. He has touched the lives of so many, making an impact wherever he goes, and in turn, God has blessed him with a long life. I am undoubtedly who I am today because such an incredible father raised me.

Carmelo Aguilar, MA, USA
My father is Carmelo Aguilar:

I had the privilege of growing up with my father present in the home, and his influence has shaped me into the man and father I am today. I watched him wake up daily and work hard to provide for our family.

I witnessed his unwavering faithfulness in serving God at church. Even during tough times, I saw him continue to trust in God. As an adult, I fully understand a father's crucial role in a child's life. My father led by example; today, I strive to lead my family similarly.

Ritta A. Opio, your loving daughter, Uganda:
Growing up as the second-to-last born and the youngest of three girls, it was no secret that my dad loved me the most. Everyone, including my siblings, knew it. He adored me so much that no one could scold, shout, or even raise a finger at me!

This made me feel incredibly special and a little untouchable. I shamelessly refused to do chores because I knew Daddy would always defend me (spoiled girl, I know!). I vividly remember how Daddy carried me from home to school every morning during my pre-primary and early primary school years. At that time, it was the only form of transport we could afford, and looking back, it is one of my fondest memories. Dad was always present throughout my education, coming to every visitation during my secondary school years.

My schoolmates thought I did not have a mother because they never saw her at visitations (not because she did not love me, but because she had to visit my older brother in another school, and the visitation days always clashed). I'll never forget how Daddy would take me back to school after visiting, walking around to greet all the teachers before finally bidding me farewell. But that was not the end.

He had always asked a few students to run to the dormitories and call me back for one last hug. That final hug always made me cry. I knew I would miss Daddy's love and pampering for the next three months. I feel so blessed to still have my old man with me. Walking me down the aisle on my wedding day was a dream. Daddy's presence and love have shaped me into who I am today. He's taught me to love, be kind, gentle, and understand.

If I were to be born again, I would not ask for any other father but this one. I could go on and on about my dad because he's my oldest, closest, and first friend, but I'll stop here. Thank you so much, Mr. James Nuwagaba, for loving me with every breath in you! You've taught me so well, and I will forever be grateful.

Simon Peter Kisakye Praise, CA, USA, precious son of the most-high God.
Experience with my dad.

On a blissful evening, as I returned to my hostel, my heart began to wonder if my daddy even knew what had happened to me that day. I had been awarded a gold medal and certificate after winning a 25K marathon competition during high school.

The thought stayed with me all night as I sat on my bed with many emotions running through my mind. I realized that throughout my entire school life, my daddy had never attended a single event or even checked on my academic performance at the end of any term or year. Yet, he always made sure to provide financially for everything I needed.

As a child, I longed for my daddy's presence at these important moments. Do not get me wrong; I was grateful for all he provided, but there was a deep desire in my heart to one day sit with him, share coffee, and proudly show him every certificate and award I had received.

Sadly, that moment never came, as his life ended, and it left a great void in my heart.

Amid this, I found comfort in the scriptures. One verse spoke deeply: *"To the fatherless, He is a father. To the widow, He is a champion friend. The lonely, He makes part of a family.*

The prisoners, He leads into prosperity until they sing for joy. This is our Holy God in His holy place! But for the rebels, there is heartache and despair." (Psalm 68:5-6, TPT)

This scripture became especially meaningful when I lost my daddy in April of 2007. Before his passing, I had noticed a significant change in his relationship with me. We were beginning to bond deeply as father and son, but his life was cut short, leaving me with an unsettled spirit, soul, and body.

However, praise be to God for His faithfulness to all men! After losing my father, I found solace in a childlike prayer.

One day, as I sat alone, wondering how I would make it through my academics, I said, "Lord God in heaven, I know you took my father and never made a wrong choice. You are the father to the fatherless. Now that I will no longer see my daddy again, I pray that you will be my father from this point on."

This prayer became my truth: ABBA FATHER is truly the BEST DADDY.

Over time, I have realized that all earthly fathers draw from God as the ultimate example. God's love has shown me how fathers should honor, imitate, and serve their children and families.

In conclusion, our generation is not left fatherless, nor are we doomed to carry the weight of the pain caused by fathers who did not know how to be present. God has risen His servants to stand in the gap.

I am one of those who celebrate the Church of Christ, for it has fathered me so well since the loss of my father. For those of us who are now fathers or those yet to establish families, God is the perfect and complete example of what it means to be a father, as ordained by Him.

Mark K., cousin, Uganda.

My father's presence provided a deep sense of security and stability. Knowing that, no matter what I pursued or what life threw at me, I had someone in my corner. His words and actions shaped me into who I am today. He instilled the values of hard work, integrity, and resilience in me.

While no one is perfect, including him, I strive to be the best version of myself through recognizing and learning from those imperfections.

Gina E., MA, USA:

I enjoyed my time with my dad while he was alive. He was very involved, caring, and committed to being a father. He loved my brother and me unconditionally. One of the last times I saw him was on December 25, 1990, when I was 5. We lived in Massachusetts, and he surprised us by visiting. I was so excited. We saw him several more times after that because he was getting sick. Eventually, he returned to Haiti, where he passed away in August 1991. I miss my dad every single day.

Losing him changed my life. Most of the responsibility fell on my mother, who was blessed and highly favored. Her village, particularly my aunt from Haiti, came to Boston to help raise us. My aunt made a huge sacrifice, leaving her family behind to choose us, and I am forever grateful for that.

Growing up without my dad was challenging. I love my mom. We are best friends, but there were times when I needed a man's advice, especially when it came to dating. Although I had male role models, having my dad around was different. I learned many lessons about men on my own. I often thought half of my challenges would not have happened if he were still here. I still feel that way.

I did not seek attention from men because my father was gone, but I gave my love to men who did not deserve it. I believe that his absence made navigating adult life harder. It wasn't easy to settle because I knew my dad and the love, he showed me in that short time set a standard. I want that kind of love he showed me. He showed me in that short time what love should look like.

I often imagine how my dad would feel knowing he has a granddaughter now and how beautiful and smart she is. It is still tough thinking about his absence, and I always think about him. While I do not feel alone, I occasionally get that empty feeling.

On a positive note, losing him strengthened my relationship with my mother. His passing made me realize at a young age that life is short and that we should learn to appreciate it. My dad died young; he was only 28. My mom became a single mother of two at 28. His death made me love her more. I am more mindful and understanding of life and deeply love her. I hold onto her because I have already lost one parent. Though I lost my dad, I gained so much. His passing helped me grow in independence and taught me always to love. You never know when to say, "See you later."

Evangelist Moses M, 35, MA, USA.

I grew up in a polygamous family. My father had three wives, and we are about 15 children, each from different districts. My mother lived in Kampala, where she struggled to care for us. Although my dad contributed financially whenever possible, it wasn't easy because he had many children to care for.

Occasionally, he would pick me up for the holidays, but once, he took me to live with my stepmother. Living with my stepmother was difficult. I wet my bed at night and would be scolded and beaten every morning for it. This happened regularly, but the worst moment came when I was around 8 or 9 years old.

One morning, I woke up completely soaked. My stepmother forced me outside, wrapped the wet sheets around my face, and whipped me in front of the neighbors. Children laughed and made fun of me, shouting, "He wets the bed!" That was my most painful day, and the trauma from it stayed with me for years. From then on, I would leave home early in the morning and return late, avoiding the other kids in the neighborhood. My confidence was shattered, and I could not bear to talk to anyone.

My dad never found out about any of this because my stepmother would only tell him good things, and I had been warned never to speak to him about what I was going through. One day, my mother realized something was wrong and came to check on me. She always thought my father had taken me to my grandmother's house. When she finally found me, I was severely ill, with a high fever, and I was alone in the house. She took me to the hospital and swore that she would not let us return to my father's care until we were much older.

The pain of not having a father present during my childhood is indescribable. I do not have any memories of moments with my dad. There were no family dinners, no vacations, and none of the things that the other kids had. While I occasionally saw him, our relationship was not deep.

I held onto bitterness, particularly toward my stepmother, and I refused to speak to her for 27 years because of how she treated me. However, as I grew in my faith, God began to teach me about forgiveness. He urged me to forgive my stepmother, even though it was a struggle. I resisted at first, always feeling that she was the one who had wronged me. Over time, I started reaching out to her, but she did not respond to my calls. Eventually, I heard that she had suffered a stroke.

Despite everything, I forgave her, whether she remembers what she did or not. I continue to pray for her, and while my relationship with my dad has improved, there is still a disconnect between us. This experience has taught me the importance of a father's role in a child's life. Even if a father is no longer with the mother, being present and active in the child's upbringing is crucial. I never had meaningful conversations about life, relationships, or important decisions with my father. I missed the chance to be guided by him, to hear about his own experiences, or to have him introduce me to mentors who could support me.

I know that many children face even worse situations, but it is still painful to have a father and not share a close relationship. Looking back, I realize how important it is for fathers to be intentional, to reach out to their children, to talk to them, and to show them love and support. Fathers should fight for their relationship with their children, regardless of the challenges they face.

The pain of growing up without a truly present father figure has shaped my resolve. Although I came from a broken family, I have decided that a broken family will not come from me. I am determined to give my children a different experience by being there for them, loving them, guiding them, and connecting with them in the ways I always longed for with my father. Amen.

Shillah K, Uganda
Growing up without a dad.

I lost my dad when I was just 2 years old, and my mom became the breadwinner, leaving my siblings and me with my grandmother while she went out to work. I thank God for always filling the gap by placing different father figures in my life at every stage.

However, deep down, I always reminded myself, "This is not your dad, so know your place in this house." This mindset made me reserved, as I never fully trusted anyone enough to open up. I was not sure how they would take it or perceive me. I constantly thought, "You're bothering them; they're just helping you. It is a privilege, not a right." As a result, I grew up denying a lot of my own needs and feelings.

This experience led me to become fiercely independent. I learned to work hard and solve my problems, meeting all my needs independently because I did not have a father who was responsible for me. At one point, I lived in a home where a man mistreated his wife, and I vowed never to get married. I told myself, "Study hard, get a good job, and care for yourself. If this is what marriage means." But I am married after a lot of deliverance and transformation by Christ in me, the Hope of Glory.

How It Impacts My Life Today: I still find it hard to ask for help or share when something bothers me. But God is helping me through my husband, who is also fathering me in many ways. He's such a good man.

Shillah L, MA USA
The Guiding Hand

My father held my hand, took that first step with me, looked into my eyes, and showed me everything would be okay. Growing up with my father has been a blessing I cherish deeply. In a household with more girls than boys, my father raised us with equal opportunities, nurturing both our femininity and masculinity. Despite cultural pressures and family comments about having more girls, he adored and valued us.

As a devout man, I recall his powerful response to a family member's remark about my mother having no heir: 'Who says a girl can't be an heir?' His words still resonate with me today. His love and support continue unabated, even now that we are grown women. He still sees us as his little girls. A father's presence is vital for both girls and boys. My father was always present, praying, playing, dancing, and engaging in meaningful conversations with us. His teaching style emphasized understanding over punishment, opting for 'table talk' instead.

While his sweetness was unmatched, his overprotectiveness sometimes felt suffocating. No school trips without him, no sleep overs, even at grandparents' homes. Only now, as a parent myself, do I understand his concerns. My mother shares stories of how he would check on us every night, asking us to leave our doors open. Today, I realize how fortunate I have been to have my father's guiding hand. His love, wisdom, and presence have shaped me into who I am today. I'm eternally grateful for the blessing of my father.

Tr. Derrick Mubiru, MN, USA:

I believe that fathers are vital in their children's lives, especially in today's world. The gap left by absent fathers has widened, particularly in Western countries. With financial pressures increasing, many fathers are too busy, leading to their absence at home.

Based on recent research I have conducted about the impact of missing fathers in homes, I have found that many fathers feel that if they provide financially by paying bills and ensuring necessities are met, they do not need to be present at home. As a result, many fathers work late into the night, missing out on their children's lives, education, and overall well-being. This absence often makes it challenging for children to build a close, foundational relationship with their fathers.

Growing up, I experienced the impact of these dynamics firsthand. My mother gave birth to me while she was still in college, and my father was also still studying. When my mother became pregnant, her parents initially sent her away from home because of her pregnancy while she was still in school. Fortunately, a few relatives intervened, offering her support during that difficult time, although it disrupted her studies.

My mother's studies came to a standstill when she had me, as she had to put her studies on hold to take care of me. I am sharing this from my research about my life at around 20 years old as I tried to understand the strife in the relationship between my paternal grandmother and my mother!

My father continued studying and pursuing mechanical engineering, which required him to spend time in various districts doing fieldwork. He was often away at large plantations, like those in Lugazi and Mityana, and my mother tried to keep up with his whereabouts, but he was constantly moving.

When I was almost a year old, my mother faced a difficult decision. She needed financial support to return to school, but her family had already distanced themselves from her. The only condition for receiving support was to leave me with my paternal family. Though it was not what she wanted, she eventually took me to my grandparents' house. My grandmother recalls coming back to find me lying on the couch, crying, with my old enough cousin trying to comfort me.

In those early years, my father was a consistent presence. He never missed a birthday and even threw birthday parties for me, which made my childhood feel special. However, when I turned nine, he passed away. That was when I truly began to experience life without a father. My father had other children from different relationships, and the demands of paying attention to his children had always been significant. I have two stepsisters and one stepbrother, each from a different mother.

This created divisions that often made it unclear where each of us fit. On my side, I had some aunts who would step in to help occasionally. Still, in today's Western culture, we do not see that level of extended family support, especially for immigrants. Here, families tend to be more nuclear; even the few extended family members are often too busy to help. Times have changed; even in Uganda, you may not get as much support because everyone is busy.

When my father died, I was in third grade, about nine years old, and my life changed significantly. My mother had gone back to school and eventually started working at an entry-level position with the Ministry of Energy. She worked tirelessly, leaving little time for me. I remember being taken to her workplace, and she would ask, "Why did you bring this child here? There is no one to look after him." It hurt to hear that because I saw other relatives, yet no one cared for me. She said they needed to take me back to my grandmother! As a result, I spent much of my childhood feeling lonely.

Growing up as a loner affected my confidence and self-esteem. I became fearful, especially of interacting with people of the opposite sex, and struggled to connect with others. Though my grandmother loved me, I still yearned for my parents' presence. My father, when alive, would only visit briefly and then leave, making me feel like I was not truly valued. This sense of abandonment and lack of consistent parental guidance left me feeling uncertain and often unable to make my own decisions. I started making my decisions when I was twenty-eight years old!

For much of my childhood and adolescence, my decisions were made by others, first by my parents and later by my grandmother and other relatives. My voice was rarely heard, which left me feeling like I was in limbo. I often felt caught in a "tug of war" between my mother and grandmother, who wanted influence over my life.

My grandmother, who raised me, would sometimes say things like, **"Olabika oyagalanyo maama wo kati, nze tokyampuliriza"** ("Now that you've grown up, you love your mother more and do not listen to me"), making it clear that she felt sidelined as I grew closer to my mother.

I always tried to balance my mother and grandmother, which was a constant challenge. When my father was alive, my mother felt she did not have full rights over me; perhaps my father's presence complicated her role. Even now, maintaining a stable relationship with my mother is difficult. Though I'm working to build a closer bond with her, it is a journey still in progress, marked by years of complex family dynamics.

Developing a close relationship with my mother has been challenging because of the many years we were apart, almost 24 to 25 years, while I lived with my grandmother. Sitting down to have deep conversations with her now can be difficult. We do catch up, but it does not feel as easy as it did with my grandmother, who was always my go-to for conversations, even about relationships.

Growing up without that open connection with my mother impacted my self-esteem and confidence, especially when I first came to the U.S., where confidence is essential. It felt like I was in a jungle, and I quickly realized I had to "man up."

On the positive side, not being overly pampered helped me grow independently. So, I grew to be a hustler because I knew where I came from. My mom often reminded me that, as a woman, she could not fully be a father figure to me. So, I found mentors who became like father figures. This taught me humility and a teachable spirit as I sought guidance from older men. When I attended Watoto Church, I connected with men who were often ten or older, helping me gain wisdom and life skills. Here in the U.S., I have started building friendships with people closer to my age, but back home, most of my friends were in their 40s and 50s. Learning from them shaped me significantly.

Not having my father around also influenced the way I approach fatherhood. I'm committed to being present in my child's life in a way I missed. I'm involved in his daily activities, like discussing football, which both of us love, talking openly about life, and making sure he feels comfortable sharing with me. I know discipline is necessary, and while I'm tough when it counts, I also prioritize bonding with him. Because I want to raise real men, I am strong on discipline and hard work! I want him to grow up seeing a father who lives by biblical principles.

Throughout my journey, I have joined fellowships and men's groups, like Men of Valor, to stay grounded and learn more about biblical manhood. Even after moving, I stay connected with men I met in Massachusetts, continuing to learn and grow. Fathers play an irreplaceable role in a child's life, offering examples and guidance that help shape their identity. Mothers are essential, but having an active, engaged father figure makes a powerful difference in a child's life.

Mothers can play a significant role, but children must learn certain aspects of manhood and decision-making from their fathers. They need to see a man's strength and resilience, especially when making life decisions and not backing down in the face of challenges. This helps a child grow into a well-rounded person, equipped with the confidence and stability that come from having both a mother's nurturing and a father's guidance.

A child raised solely by a mother may make more emotionally driven decisions, as women naturally have a nurturing, emotional side. However, men tend to approach decisions more factually, focusing on practical realities. Children need to experience this balance and understand the importance of facing facts, like the responsibility to work and provide for their families.

They need to see a father figure who embodies strength and faith, someone who acknowledges his responsibilities and acts on them. Personally, the experiences around me have helped me grow past my emotions and stand firmly as a man. With the support of other men, I have gained a stronger foundation in faith and purpose. Thank you for allowing me to share my story. Shalom, and God bless you!

Fortunate L, Manchester, UK:

If I could stay in school, nothing else really mattered. My only goal was to finish, even though I was not sure it would be possible. I decided I'd study as long as possible, and if school fees ran out, I'd stay home and figure something else out, as there was no one else to help.

Growing up, my dad provided everything we needed, even though he was not wealthy. When I got to high school, he became ill, and then he passed away. That changed everything for my siblings and me. After that, I stopped expecting visits on school visitation days like the other students. Still, those days were hard, reminding me of everything I'd lost. But I kept pushing forward.

Finances became a constant struggle, especially with school fees. I was often sent home, missing exams or returning late and falling behind. By senior four, I was losing hope of finishing. A kind teacher eventually spoke to the headmistress, convincing her to cover half my fees since I was on the sports team. That helped, though finding the other half was still difficult.

In senior five, I returned to school late and missed important lessons, which affected my grades. I told myself I'd keep going, no matter what. When it came to university, I did not know if I'd make it. If that did not work out, I thought I'd try hands-on training, though I had no clear plan.

Losing my dad left a big gap, especially in my education. I felt his absence deeply, not only in school but in the basics that were hard to ask for. My uncle stepped in to help, but he was not the type to check in; I had to speak up if needed. So, I relied on my cousins and siblings for clothes and essentials. They shared what they could, and I got by, but it took work.

Psychologically, I coped by accepting things as they were. I knew nothing would come easily, and I'd have to figure it out alone. I pushed forward, realizing that if help came, great, but I could not depend on it.

The hardest part was taking responsibility for my younger siblings. No one else was willing to step in, even though my dad had helped raise some relatives who did not ultimately come through for us. That weight has been tough to carry. I was somewhat grown when my dad passed, so I have made peace with it, though the void will always remain. Every child deserves both parents, yet life does not always work that way.

My sister struggled, especially with her severe health issues, which began around the same time my dad got sick, and she never fully recovered. Losing our dad broke something in her, and she could not handle the reality like I could. My brother fell off, too, as he still struggles to accept the reality we live in! It hit all of us differently!

My dad's absence impacts many aspects of life, especially family traditions. I still need to involve my dad's side of the family when I have significant events. I balance honoring his memory and handling relatives who may not fully understand my life. My uncle has done his part, and I appreciate him for stepping up, though we do not talk about personal matters the way I could with my mom.

Conclusion

Wow, I am deeply moved by these stories from my friends. It makes me wonder what your child would write about you as their parent. What would they say about the father they no longer see? I can't even imagine what I would have written about my dad during those difficult times or what my sister would have written about him. In many stories, we see children with absent parents facing serious challenges and learning to be resilient and independent. Dr. Myles Munroe once said, **"Live well today so you won't be afraid of your memories."** What memories do you carry of your dad? What memories will your children carry of you?

These experiences reveal how deeply children need their fathers and a father figure in their lives, as much as they need their mothers. They make me agree with Dr. Myles Munroe, who said, ***"If you do not/will not take the responsibility of raising them, do not reproduce***

them." I know we can't control some events in life, like death, but whatever we get to do, let us do it diligently.

All these stories touch me deeply, and I'm incredibly thankful to my friends for sharing them. I feel particularly overwhelmed by Fortunate's story; we've been friends since our first year of high school. We went through high school and studied French together, but I never knew her full story. I noticed she rarely had visitors on visiting day, but I never asked why. When she shared her story for this book, I felt overwhelmed and even asked her if I had been kind to her in school. It made me realize how important it is to be kind to everyone because we often have no idea what people are enduring.

Honestly, what could I have done but share the little I had since my mom was also struggling? She gave us everything she had and could. Many kids, unfortunately, fall out of school for similar reasons, but Fortunate carried herself with such grace. I never once saw her cry over not being visited, though I know I would have! She focused on her studies, stayed out of trouble, and went on to become a chemical engineer. She learned to be independent, and I could not be prouder of the person she is today. Her daughter, Jazmine, is truly blessed to have such a remarkable mother.

Above all, we can only do our best, but we would still be insufficient. All our needs can only be satisfied by one greater. Only a relationship with Jesus Christ meets our core needs for acceptance, identity, and purpose. So, I pray that we all do not miss to know Him personally.

This book is a conversation starter, and many of you will rise to speak up on the topics discussed. Mothers and fathers, I do not want your child to go through life like I have. It is tough; it is so heavy. Let us step up and work to be the parents our generation needs, whether as mothers, fathers, aunties, uncles, or mentors. Our generation is calling for us. Let us answer.

> *"Fatherhood is a joy; it shouldn't be anything less."*
> *- Pastor Tom Kiessling at Photizo Daily*

God, Our Perfect Father

As I have shared, the word "father" carried no significance in my life for a long time. It felt like an empty title, devoid of warmth, security, or trust. Because of this, I struggled to relate to God as a Father. I believed in Him, loved Him, and knew He cared for me, but my relationship with Him as a Father was blurry and distant, like trying to hold on to something you've never truly experienced.

As my pastor said, when fathers are absent or abusive, they defile their children's understanding of God as a Father. They create a warped lens through which we view authority, care, and love. If your earthly father did not show up or cause you harm, it is no wonder you might find it hard to trust God as your heavenly Father. That was my reality for years. I believed in God, but trusting Him as my Father? I had to learn that, and I'm still learning it.

Yet, God, in His love and patience, has been teaching me what true fatherhood looks like. He's been teaching me to trust Him with my heart, needs, and future. I know many of us who have not had fathers present or who've endured hurtful relationships with them, and I want to introduce you to one: God, the father to the Fatherless. *"A father to the fatherless, a defender of widows, is God in his holy dwelling."* (Psalm 68:5, NIV)

My Kenyan friend, Dorah, shared her story at Photizo Daily. She lost her father as a teenager, and his absence left a deep void in her heart. She tried to fill that void with many things, but nothing satisfied her. Then, one day, God spoke to her and said, "I am your Father. You do not have an earthly father, but I am your father. I can do everything you want your father to do and even more."

From that moment on, Dorah's life changed. She said the emptiness was filled, and she found true satisfaction in God. Now, whenever she needs guidance, provision, or comfort, she goes to Him, asks, and He answers. That is who God is, a Father who listens, provides, and loves without condition. It is true! God answers when we call on Him and says it in His word.

He wants all of us to know Him that way. When He sent Jesus to die for us, it was not just to save us from sin; it was to redeem us and bring us into His family as children.

As human beings, we are insufficient in so many ways. We are prone to failure, doubt, and brokenness. But God is all-sufficient. He lacks nothing. In Him, we have everything we could ever need. As I continually learn to relate to Him as my Father, I find that my endless quest for fulfillment and belonging diminishes. The ache of wanting something more fades, and my gaze shifts completely to Him.

He is the true end to the endless quest. He is perfect, faithful, and all-satisfying. Day by day, I'm learning to trust Him more deeply. With each step I take toward Him, I discover a Father who can meet my needs and surpass all my expectations.

To parents reading this, I urge you to introduce your children to this God early. Teach them about the only Father who truly satisfies. Let them see you pray and depend on Him. While human fathers are critical, only God is perfect. Only God can fill the deepest voids in our hearts. If you teach your children to find their identity in Him early, they won't search for it in men, women, or places they cannot satisfy. Yes, human guidance and relationships are crucial, but knowing God is eternal life.

God's love is not a concept; it is a reality. He longs to embrace you as His child. Will you let Him? Whether you're a parent seeking to raise your children well or someone still yearning for a father's love, God is here for you. He has always been. He will never fail, abandon, or abuse you. He is our perfect Father.

He is ABBA. Amen.

"Even if my father and mother abandon me, the Lord will hold me close." (Psalm 27:10, NLT)

Further Study: Mathew 6:33, Romans 8:15, 1 John 3:1.

EPILOGUE 2

INSPIRATION FOR FATHERS

I can't share everything, but Dr. Myles Munroe is another great person who has profoundly impacted me through his teachings. If you haven't already, I encourage you to watch his videos on YouTube or read his books on fatherhood. His insights are invaluable, especially for men. Mothers, share these lessons with your sons. Ladies, gift your husbands something truly meaningful beyond socks...hahaha. by buying them constructive books.

I have committed to listening to Dr. Munroe's sermons almost daily, and they've transformed my life. Though he's no longer with us, his legacy as a mentor continues to shape my views, particularly on fatherhood and relationships. He was a strong advocate for men stepping up, teaching, and leading, and I pray more men follow in his footsteps. His teachings on leadership, manhood, and family dynamics have reshaped my life. Ladies, you'll benefit from his wisdom, too.

Here's a brief overview of his essential works:

Understanding the Purpose and Power of Men: This book emphasizes the role of men as fathers and leaders, highlighting their God-given responsibility to be visionaries, providers, and protectors.

The Fatherhood Principle: A deep dive into the divine purpose of fatherhood, explaining how fathers are the foundation of their families, shaping their children's identities and futures.

The Power of Character in Leadership: This book explores how a father's character directly affects his ability to lead and guide his family, emphasizing integrity and moral strength.

The Principles and Power of Vision: Focused on leadership and purpose, this book explains how fathers provide direction and help their children discover their God-given potential.

These teachings collectively showcase Dr. Munroe's powerful vision of men as leaders, protectors, and nurturers within the family.

Since I enjoy making notes, I have written down key points from his sermons.

- ✶ Everything a parent does shapes their children's identity unless God intervenes.

- ✶ Love goes beyond the gifts you give your children; it is about giving them your presence. When God loved the world, He did not send gifts; He sent Himself through Jesus. If you can't give of yourself, think twice about bringing children into the world.

- ✶ Some children are desperate for correction, but some fathers do not see it. Fathers must correct, reprove, and guide their children, showing them the way they should go.

- ✶ Do not leave the raising of your children to teachers or allow them to raise themselves; God entrusted you with that responsibility.

- ★ Your role is not to curse but to warn and encourage.
- ★ Many of society's issues can often be traced back to fathers.

Quotes That Define Fathers and Their Influence

"One father is more than a hundred schoolmasters."
—George Herbert, Anglican priest and poet

"A good father is one of the most unsung, unpraised, unnoticed, and yet one of the most valuable assets in our society."
—Billy Graham, American evangelist and writer

"All great change in America begins at the dinner table."
—Ronald Reagan, Former U.S. President

"Fathering is a marathon, a long and often trying journey, and we must be disciplined if we hope to finish successfully."
—Ken Canfield, National Center for Fatherhood

"A man who wants to lead the orchestra must turn his back on the crowd. Likewise, a father must sometimes choose the road less traveled to lead his family."
–Max Lucado

"A father's influence on his children is powerful, and his primary duty is to reflect Christ to them in everything he does."
–John MacArthur

"Fathers, your primary responsibility is to introduce your children to God through the way you love and lead them."
–James Dobson

"A father's legacy is not just in what he does for his children, but in the spiritual inheritance he leaves by guiding them toward Christ."
–Henry Blackaby

"A good father is one of the most unsung, unpraised, unnoticed, and yet one of the most valuable assets in our society."
–Billy Graham

"Fatherhood is the ultimate responsibility of a man. The destiny of nations rests on the shoulders of fathers."
–Dr. Myles Munroe

"A godly father is a man who understands his weaknesses, embraces his responsibilities, and seeks God's grace for the journey."
–Paul Washer

"Fatherhood is not just a position but a mission. God has entrusted children to us to lead, love, and nurture toward Him."
–David Platt

"A father's absence challenges traditional ideas of masculinity."
Source unknown

EPILOGUE 3

LET US PRAY FOR FATHERHOOD AND THE FATHERLESS

Dear Heavenly Father,
We come before You with a heart full of gratitude for the gift of fatherhood. Thank You for the fathers who have stepped up to love, nurture, and guide their children, reflecting Your love and care in their lives. I pray for all fathers today that they may seek Your wisdom and strength in their roles. May they be sources of support and encouragement, instilling confidence and security in their children. Help them to reflect Your love through their actions and words.
Lord, I also lift those who have experienced fatherlessness. I ask for Your healing touch for those who feel the absence of a father figure. Fill the void left by their earthly fathers with Your unfailing love and presence. May they know they are never alone, for You are their ultimate Father, always present, loving, and ready to listen.
We pray for single mothers who bear the weight of parenting alone. Grant them strength, patience, and resilience as they raise their children without a partner. Surround them with support and encouragement from family, friends, and community. May they find solace in knowing they are not alone in their journey, and may they lean on you for guidance and provision. Help them nurture their children with love and grace, instilling the values and lessons they need to flourish.
Grant those struggling with feelings of abandonment, rejection, or hurt the grace to forgive and release the pain they carry. Help them to understand their worth in Your eyes and to see themselves as beloved children. May they find comfort in knowing that You have a purpose and a plan for their lives.
Father, I pray for the struggling fathers, whether due to their wounds or life circumstances. Please give them the strength to overcome challenges, to seek healing, and to break the cycle of hurt. Surround them with support and guidance so they can lead their families with love and integrity.
As we navigate the complexities of fatherhood and fatherlessness, help us remember the importance of connection, communication, and compassion. May we all strive to build relationships that honor You, creating nurturing environments for our children to thrive.
In Jesus's name, we pray.

Amen.

CONCLUSION

CALL TO ACTION

This book is a conversation starter, and I know there is more! However, I am deeply committed to sharing and discussing the themes explored in ***Endless Quest: Where Is My Dad At?*** This book reflects my journey and a call to address the fatherlessness prevalent in our generation! Discover emotional healing and restoration that has helped me!

Whether speaking to individuals, families, churches, or organizations, my passion is to delve deeper into these vital topics to inspire healing, transformation, and hope.

Please reach out if you'd like to invite me to speak or connect further!

Contact information:
    Email: Vivienneoflove@gmail.com
Follow me on Instagram, Facebook, Twitter, TikTok, and YouTube @ Vivienne D'amour.

Let us journey together toward healing, wholeness, and discovering God's perfect fatherhood.

ABOUT THE AUTHOR

Vivian Nabakembo adopted the name Vivienne D'amour during her high school French days. The name, which means "Vivian of Love," originated from a simple moment when her French teacher began calling her Vivienne. She found it to be fancy and unique, especially since she was learning French for the first time. With several girls in her school sharing her name, three of them in her class, she decided to make Vivienne her own.

As her love for the French language grew, she added "D'amour," feeling it captured her essence perfectly. She says, "Love has always been at the core of my being. I was made for love and to love."

She often laughs when recalling how, after her first term of French class, she proudly declared at home that she could now teach French. Looking back, she realizes how little she knew at the time, but her enthusiasm was undeniable.

That same enthusiasm, passion for learning and sharing knowledge have remained defining aspects of Vivienne.

Today, she shares not out of excitement or a sense of expertise, but because she believes it's essential.

Vivienne published her first book at the age of 12. While she planned to continue writing through high school, an unfinished manuscript from a school vacation remained untouched. Though she excelled in English composition, her growing fascination with French eventually shifted her focus from English literature to deepening her language skills.

Over the years, Vivienne has shared heartfelt reflections on life through stories posted on her Facebook. Though she stepped away from formal writing during a period when reading didn't capture her interest, knowing writers are also avid readers, she now recognizes how God has a way of drawing us back to our true purpose.

Four years ago, Vivienne received divine inspiration to write *Endless Quest*, a book that reflects on her experience of growing up with an absent father. Through this work, she emphasizes the critical need for fathers in today's world, highlighting their crucial role in children's emotional and spiritual development and advocating for their presence in nurturing future generations.

Vivienne holds a bachelor's degree in business statistics from Makerere University, Uganda. She serves as a prayer leader in her church, hosts a Christian talk show, and is the founder and CEO of Photizo Daily, a Christian media platform. Additionally, she is a certified Network Associate. Passionate about innovation, Vivienne is actively advancing her skills in cybersecurity, continually growing both personally and professionally.

Endless Quest is her debut book as an adult, marking a transformative journey of growth, faith, and self-discovery. Through her experiences, lessons, and research, she offers insights she believes her generation can relate to, inspiring the learning and unlearning necessary to build stronger families for the future.

Made in the USA
Middletown, DE
17 March 2025